YORK NOTES

General Editors: Professor A.N. Jeffares (*University of Stirling*) & Professor Suheil Bushrui (*American University of Beirut*)

John Steinbeck

OF MICE AND MEN

Notes by Martin Stephen

BA (LEEDS) PH D (SHEFFIELD)
Second Master, Sedbergh School

LONGMAN
YORK PRESS

YORK PRESS
Immeuble Esseily, Place Riad Solh, Beirut.

LONGMAN GROUP UK LIMITED
Longman House, Burnt Mill, Harlow,
Essex CM20 2JE, England
Associated companies, branches and representatives
throughout the world

First published 1980
Tenth impression 1993

ISBN 0-582-03091-9

Produced by Longman Singapore Publishers Pte Ltd
Printed in Singapore

Contents

Part 1: Introduction *page* 5
   The life of John Steinbeck   5
   The work of John Steinbeck   9
   The literary and historical background   10
   A note on the text   12

Part 2: Summaries   13
   A general summary   13
   Detailed summaries   14

Part 3: Commentary   30
   The title   30
   Plot and structure   30
   Themes   32
   Characterisation   39
   Style   48

Part 4: Hints for study   52
   Points to select for detailed study   52
   Quotations   53
   Effective arrangement of material   56
   Planning an answer   57
   Specimen answers   60
   Questions   68

Part 5: Suggestions for further reading   69

The author of these notes   71

Part 1

Introduction

The life of John Steinbeck

John Ernst Steinbeck was born on 27 February 1902, in Salinas, California. He was the third of four children, and of mixed German and Irish descent. His parents owned a considerable amount of land, but by American standards were not particularly rich. Steinbeck's mother was a schoolteacher, and encouraged him in his natural inclination to read widely, but there was nothing very remarkable about his childhood. Later on in his life stories were to circulate in Salinas about his poverty as a child, and his promise as a writer and observer of human nature, but these were largely exaggerations, designed to fulfil a need for the 'rags-to-riches' story that people found so attractive. He attended Salinas High School, graduating from there in 1919, and having achieved minor sporting distinction as well as contributing quite frequently to the school magazine.

Steinbeck then attended Stanford University, with marine biology as his major subject. All through his life he had a deep interest in the workings of the natural world, and this is reflected in his books, many of which contain minutely detailed descriptions of nature. Certainly he was apparently more interested in nature and literature than he was in following a formal course of study. He had to take long periods away from the university in order to work and thus gain money for the continuation of his studies. He held a bewildering variety of part-time and temporary jobs, including working as a ranch-hand near King City (an experience he was to draw upon later when writing *Of Mice and Men*), and was at various times employed as a clerk, a shop assistant, a waiter, and a labourer. Perhaps his strangest job was 'breaking army remounts for officers' gentle behinds': he had to take the semi-wild horses bought by the United States Army and render them fit to be ridden by officers. He received thirty dollars for the basic training, fifty if he put the horses through the training necessary to allow them to be used in the game of polo, and a limp which he said was to last him for months. Throughout his life he had a deep love of horses and dogs.

He contributed several short stories to the Stanford University magazine, the *Spectator*, but left in 1925 without taking a degree, and went to New York, determined to be a writer. It was a brave decision. His parents had wanted him to be a lawyer, and obtaining his degree would have given him a secure and rewarding job for life. Acting as he did, he had no financial reserves (to get to New York he had to work his way as a seaman aboard a merchant ship) and no professional experience. It was ten years before he had any real success, and in those ten years his resolution to be a writer was tested to the utmost.

He went to New York with high hopes; he left it an apparent failure. He had difficulty in getting a job, but eventually worked on a building site in Madison Avenue. Then a relative used his influence to get him a job as a reporter, but he was dismissed within a short while, and he left New York after only a year, the same way that he had arrived, working his passage on a freighter. From 1926 to 1928 he based himself on the West Coast, in particular round the Lake Tahoe area, taking whatever jobs came his way; at varying times he was employed as a caretaker, a mail-coach driver, and worked in the local fish hatchery. It was here, in 1928, that he met his first wife, Carol Henning. She had come to Lake Tahoe as a tourist, and met Steinbeck when being shown round the fish hatchery. Steinbeck moved to San Francisco, where Carol had a job. They were married in 1930.

Steinbeck's first novel, *Cup of Gold*, was rejected seven times before it finally found a publisher in 1929. A fictionalised account of the buccaneer Sir Henry Morgan, it was a financial failure. Steinbeck's father probably did more than anyone else to keep Steinbeck sane and still writing at this time. When John and his new wife moved to the Monterey Peninsula, Steinbeck's father allowed them to use the family's summer cottage as their home, rent free. He also gave his son an allowance of twenty-five dollars a month to live on, supplemented by whatever Carol could earn. The future must have seemed bleak; Steinbeck had received scant praise and even less money for *Cup of Gold*, and was having great difficulty finding a publisher for his recent work.

1931 saw a turning point in Steinbeck's career, when the firm of McIntosh and Otis agreed to act as his literary agents, a relationship which was to continue for forty years. Steinbeck's abiding gratitude to this firm was shown much later in 1962, when he was awarded the Nobel Prize for Literature. The award brought with it a considerable sum of money, and Steinbeck insisted that McIntosh and Otis take a percentage of this, just as if the award had been a contract which they had obtained for him. In 1932 the firm found a publisher for Steinbeck's novel *Pastures of Heaven*; typically, Steinbeck wrote to a friend, 'They have palmed off the Pastures on somebody.' He was always extremely modest, and even dismissive, about his own work. Also in 1932 he came to know Edward F. Ricketts, a marine biologist, philosopher, and ecologist, who was to become one of his closest friends and collaborators.

The tide of events seemed to be turning in Steinbeck's favour, but despite this the next two or three years were not happy ones. *To A God Unknown* was published in 1933, but the depression had hit the United States, and Steinbeck's publishers were financially insecure, on the brink of bankruptcy. In addition, both his mother and his father were seriously ill; his mother died in 1934, his father in 1936. It was the illness of his father that hit Steinbeck especially hard. His mother, paralysed, took a year to die, but his father took even longer, and for his last two or three years was a desperately unhappy and senile old man, physically incapable and mentally stagnant.

Steinbeck's first real success was the novel *Tortilla Flat*, published in 1935. *Of Mice and Men*, published in 1937, was even more of a commercial success. Both books were eventually made into films, but *Of Mice and Men* was also dramatised, and won a Drama Critics' Award. It was made the monthly selection of the Book-of-the-Month Club, which guaranteed it wide publicity and huge sales. Steinbeck loved to travel, and a portion of the money from his two successful novels went into financing a trip he made with migrant workers to California; this was to form the basis of what is still probably his best-known work, *The Grapes of Wrath*, which was published in 1939 and was awarded the prestigious Pulitzer Prize in 1940. It too was made into a highly successful film. Steinbeck had written to the publishers of *The Grapes of Wrath* before publication warning them to print only a small number of copies; he prophesied, 'This will not be a successful book.' It is generally recognised today as one of the best novels to have emerged from the United States this century.

Success seems to have altered Steinbeck little; it removed financial worry, but replaced it with others. He was now a public figure, but disliked the adulation that his position brought him, and worried that flattery might somehow reduce his powers as a novelist. He was soon receiving up to seventy-five letters a day, some of them abusive (a Mr Lemuel Gadberry wrote to him saying that he had felt degraded after reading *Of Mice and Men*, and cheated of two dollars), and being besieged by autograph hunters and people begging for money. A girl he had known in childhood accused him, falsely, of fathering her child, an accusation which caused him much pain. Steinbeck, always a lonely man, struggled to maintain his balance and artistic integrity in the new world into which his success had brought him. He was more able to deal with the criticisms launched at his books, in particular *The Grapes of Wrath*. Right-wing elements and rich farmers protested stridently that he was a dangerous revolutionary, a Communist, a Jewish sympathiser, and a liar, none of which were true, whilst left-wing elements damned him for daring to state that man could achieve dignity and self-respect in impossible economic conditions, and condemned him for not demanding revolution. So heated was the debate that the playwright Edward Albee, a friend of Steinbeck's, wrote to him to warn of possible attempts on his life. Steinbeck dismissed the threats stoically; his life up to this point had taught him how to bear adverse criticism much more easily than praise.

However, further personal problems were coming his way. In 1940 he had been to Hollywood and met a professional singer called Gwendolyn Conger. He fell in love with her, and his marriage to Carol began to disintegrate. He suffered much before he finally divorced Carol and married Gwendolyn in 1942. He was later to say that his marriage to Carol was the story of two people who hurt each other for eleven years, but this was probably an exaggeration uttered in the heat of the moment. He never lost touch completely with Carol, asked after her in letters to friends, and was deeply touched when she was one of the first people to write to him on the occasion of his winning his Nobel Prize. Unfortunately, this second marriage was even shorter than his first. Gwendolyn bore him two sons, Thomas in 1944 and John in 1946, but signs of strain were becoming evident in the marriage by 1944, and in 1948 Gwendolyn obtained a divorce on the grounds of incompatibility. The early bitterness of the break-up seems to have dissolved after a while, and Steinbeck was allowed relatively free access to his sons.

Meanwhile he was heavily occupied in the Second World War, from about 1941 to its end in 1945. He wrote propaganda for the government, and became a war correspondent for the *New York Herald Tribune*; he had a film, *Lifeboat*, directed by Alfred Hitchcock, and became involved with him and Twentieth Century-Fox in a fierce dispute over what Steinbeck saw as distortions of his original script.

The year 1948 was another climactic year; apart from his divorce, he lost his greatest friend Edward Ricketts, who was killed when his car was hit by a train, and this accident plunged him into a deep depression. But in 1950 he married his third wife, Elaine Scott, a divorcee who had been working in Hollywood. Of her he wrote, 'It is the first peace I have had with a woman', and this marriage was to prove by far the most successful of the three.

Critics and readers are continually re-discovering forgotten novels by Steinbeck and hailing them as masterpieces, but it is probably true to say that after 1943 he only produced three novels that are still widely read today—*Cannery Row* (1944), *East of Eden* (1952), and *The*

Winter of Our Discontent (1961). Nevertheless, he was far from inactive. He travelled widely, and visited Russia and the Iron Curtain countries on the suggestion of the American government. He saw his eldest son go off to fight in the Vietnam war, and went out there himself as a war correspondent. He developed warm relationships with three Presidents of the United States—Theodore Roosevelt, Lyndon B. Johnson, and John F. Kennedy—and an almost random selection of some of the people he met and knew would include film stars, politicians and princesses, with motor car magnates and film producers. He became fascinated by *Le Morte Darthur*, a fifteenth-century version of the legend of King Arthur and the Knights of the Round Table written by the Englishman Sir Thomas Malory (d.1471), and did much research in England for an uncompleted modern version of the story, which Steinbeck saw as having great relevance to modern-day society. He was awarded the Nobel Prize for Literature in 1962, and died of heart disease in 1968. He was buried in Salinas, California.

Steinbeck was a modest, lonely man, given to moods of black depression, and never at peace with himself. He was never content with his work, always seeking the next step forward and restlessly searching for the final expression of his art. His letters manifest a great love of animals and outdoor pursuits; what is equally obvious from his books is that beneath this lay an even deeper love of humanity, especially the plain working man, born out of a clear understanding of his strengths and weaknesses.

The work of John Steinbeck

For some years now it has been fashionable to sneer gently at the work of Steinbeck, and dismiss him as not being a writer of the first rank. If the decision about his greatness and stature as a writer had been left to the professional critics, then he would probably by now have been regarded as a moderately worthwhile but essentially minor talent. The criticisms are not hard to find. Even Steinbeck's most ardent admirers would not deny that his non-fiction work is uninspiring. He has been accused of sentimentality, uneven style, melodrama, and muddled thinking. He has been described as a 'regional' novelist, a man capable of writing only about certain small areas of his own country, and thereby limited in his scope. It has been said also that his work is shallow, seeking at heart only to comfort the reader, and not challenge his basic preconceptions or stimulate him to thought. Conservatives have criticised his works as being Communist, whilst Communists have damned him for not demanding the revolution. It has been said that his work lacks real thought, and is designed for a readership who want the appearance of a novel for intellectuals, but not its content.

Two things have stopped this view of Steinbeck's work from achieving total dominance. The first is a small band of critics who have steadfastly refused to accept Steinbeck as anything less than one of the greatest twentieth-century American writers. More telling has been the influence of the reading public, who have continued to buy and read his novels in vast quantities. His work has been translated into almost every major world language, and a modern paperback edition of *Of Mice and Men* such as that issued by Pan Books has gone through no less than six printings in only four years. Possibly as a result of overwhelming public support Steinbeck has now begun to receive a much kinder press, and his reputation as one of America's greatest novelists now seems secure.

Steinbeck is known above all by two of his novels—*Of Mice and Men* (1937), and *The Grapes of Wrath* (1939)—and the latter is essential reading for any student of his work. He wrote many other novels, and any selection from them is bound to be open to criticism. Of the shorter works, the best-known are *Tortilla Flat* (1935), *Cannery Row* (1945), and *The Pearl* (1947); all are short, and very readable. Of the longer novels, the most worthwhile are probably *East of Eden* (1952) and *The Winter of Our Discontent* (1961). Also very worthwhile is *Journal of a Novel: The 'East of Eden' Letters*; published in 1969 after his death, this is an account of his feelings and thoughts whilst writing *East of Eden*, written at the same time as he was writing the novel. It is arguably more interesting than the novel itself.

Steinbeck's work cannot be classified into neat categories; his mind ranged too far and wide for that to be possible. There are not great intellectual surprises in his work, but there is a deep and abiding sympathy for ordinary men and women. His literary skills include the accurate and evocative presentation of colloquial and vernacular speech, the ability to describe nature in simple terms that yet manage to gain symbolic overtones, a great sense of drama and climax, and the ability to describe very vividly the tensions and relationships that exist within a tightly knit group of people. Perhaps one of his greatest skills is an ability to create an atmosphere, be it that of the bunk-house, the migrant camp, or the dawn over the Salinas River.

The literary and historical background

The 1920s are sometimes referred to as the 'Lost Generation' period in American literature. American involvement in the First World War (1914–18) had embittered many artists and intellectuals, who were disgusted by the materialism, extravagance, and narrow-mindedness that they thought dominated American society. In particular they hated what they saw as the smugness and unquestioning obedience to outdated and inadequate codes of behaviour that seemed to typify much of American society. Large numbers of American writers and artists went to Paris, forming an expatriate colony there. In general the 'Lost Generation' writers were hostile towards American society, satirical, and rebellious. Sinclair Lewis (1885–1951), whose best-known novel is *Babbit* (1922), Sherwood Anderson (1876–1941), and Ernest Hemingway (1898–1961) are some of the better-known writers of this period. The 1920s were also a boom time. Whilst there was vast poverty in the country, there was also vast wealth. Share values were climbing to unprecedented heights on the Wall Street Stock Exchange, and there was a frantic hurry to invest and share in the wealth that at last seemed to be available to everybody. The 1920s also marked the rise of the great gangsters; the Government had brought in Prohibition, an attempt to ban or at least severely restrict the sale of alcohol. The measure did nothing to stop the popular demand for alcoholic drinks, and organised crime stepped in to fill this need. Loathsome and perverted as the crime syndicates may have been, ironically they often performed a vital social function, in that they were often the only agencies to bother with the vast immigrant ghettoes that were forming in the major American cities. One novelist who caught the peculiar blend of extravagance and corruption that was prevalent at the time was F. Scott Fitzgerald (1896–1940), whose novel *The Great Gatsby* is the classic of its time.

All this was to change with startling rapidity. Share prices plummeted in 1929, and for the next ten years the western industrialised nations were caught in the grip of a world-wide economic depression, without the economic knowledge necessary for changing the situation, and with no machinery for coping with the vast numbers of people who found themselves unemployed and with no way of supporting either themselves or their families. It was not only industry that was hit; demand for all goods decreased, and farmers in particular were hard-hit. Unprecedented droughts hit some parts of the nation. The small farmers who worked the land lacked modern farming methods and machinery; drought and bad farming techniques led to the loss of top-soil from the fields, and the creation of vast 'dust-bowls' in what had once been productive land. Poor crops meant that the farmers were unable to pay back the money they had borrowed to buy the land in the first place, or were unable to support themselves on the meagre products of their land. They were evicted, or left of their own accord, and joined the vast tide of migration to the western states, especially California, where there was rumoured to be prosperity and wealth for all. The rumours were ill-founded; California and the surrounding states were soon choked with migrants, and conditions were no better for them than they had been in their original homes, or were much worse. It is this migration that is pictured in Steinbeck's *The Grapes of Wrath*.

By about 1937, the situation was changing for the better. President Roosevelt, more by accident than by design, had hit on some of the measures necessary to jerk the nation out of economic depression. His 'New Deal' poured thousands of millions of dollars into the ailing economy to stimulate demand and avert the very real threat of total social disintegration. Nevertheless, the process of recovery was to prove long and arduous. The novels of the thirties are often different in tone from those of the twenties, and reflect the economic collapse and the suffering it brought in its trail. Anger gives way to sympathy, and a search after the reasons behind social and economic collapse replaces satirical attack. The novelist James T. Farrell (*b.*1904) made his name with a series of novels on the Chicago poor, and though different in many ways, *The Grapes of Wrath* is generally recognised as belonging to the same 'proletarian literature' group as Farrell's work. A different group was composed of authors such as William Faulkner (1897–1962) and Thomas Wolfe (1900–36), who, whilst not ignoring social problems, tended to write more regional work, that is books whose stories and characters are based firmly on one particular area.

It would be wrong to classify Steinbeck as simply one of the 'proletarian writers'; his concern for poor people is evident, but whatever his accusers may have said, he does little social probing; it is not the reasons for human behaviour that concern him so much as its actualities. Similarly, he is in part a regional novelist, in that the area around the Salinas River is described frequently in his novels, but it is not the region that is the mainspring of his inspiration. It may be the background of a novel, but the foreground is occupied by people who are human enough to have come from almost any area.

A note on the text

Of Mice and Men was first published by William Heinemann, London, 1937, and by Viking Press, New York, 1937.

There are no textual problems with Steinbeck's works. The best edition for the majority of students is that issued by Pan Books, in association with William Heinemann (London, 1974). Sixteen other titles by Steinbeck are also available in the same series.

Part 2

Summaries

of OF MICE AND MEN

A general summary

One warm evening, two men walk down from the highway to a pool by the Salinas River. George is small, dark, and moves quickly, whilst it soon becomes apparent that Lennie, huge and blank-faced, is half-witted. They are off to take up work on a nearby ranch, but George tells Lennie not to say a word when they arrive; they have had to leave their previous job for some unspecified reason to do with Lennie. Before they go to sleep, Lennie makes George tell him a story he has obviously heard many times before, how when they get a little money together they will run a small farm, with rabbits and other animals on it for Lennie to look after. They start work at the farm, and meet Curley, the violent and argumentative son of the ranch owner, who has recently married a girl who is already showing signs of wanting to be unfaithful to him. Frightened that there will be trouble between Curley and Lennie, George arranges to meet Lennie by the pool where they spent the previous night, if there is any trouble. They meet Slim, the chief horse and mule driver, and a man with natural authority. Talking to him, George reveals that they were 'run out' of Weed, where they had previously been working, when Lennie was wrongly accused of trying to rape a girl. Lennie is given a young puppy, and Carlson, a farm-hand, makes Candy, an old man who cleans up round the farm, let his old dog be shot, because it smells and is too old to be of any further use. Depressed over the loss of his dog, Candy hears George telling Lennie about their plan for a little farm, and offers to put up half the money if they will let him come in with them. Curley breaks in, and starts a fight with Lennie, but after taking a battering, Lennie crushes Curley's hand; Slim makes Curley say that his hand was injured in an accident in a machine. One evening when nearly everyone has gone out to the local town, Lennie enters Crooks's hut; Crooks is a crippled and embittered negro who works on the farm in the stables. Lennie and Candy tell Crooks about their plan for a farm, but they are interrupted by Curley's wife, who threatens Crooks with a false rape charge when she is asked to leave the hut. Later Lennie kills the pup he has been given, not knowing his own strength, and while he is trying to bury it in the straw that lies on the floor of the barn Curley's wife comes in. They talk, and she asks him to stroke her hair. She panics when she feels Lennie's strength, and by accident Lennie breaks her neck. When the body is found, it is obvious that Lennie is the murderer, and a hunt is started for him. Deciding that Lennie could not bear life in prison, and that he does not want him lynched by the farm-hands, George goes to where he knows Lennie will be, and shoots him. Only Slim understands why he had to do this.

Detailed summaries

There are no chapter divisions in *Of Mice and Men*, but there are a number of readily recognisable sections to the book, and most texts leave a clear line between them. The section numbers will not be found in the text, but for reference purposes page numbers are given for each section from the Pan edition, and the first line of each section is supplied to enable the student to find them more easily.

Section 1. Pages 7–20: *'A few miles south of Soledad, the Salinas River . . . '*

SUMMARY: The book opens with a description of the country around the Salinas River, south of Soledad. Two men come down to a pool by the river from the highway; George is small and dark, Lennie huge and ponderous. Lennie drinks from the stagnant water of the pool, and is told off for doing so by George. The two men are heading for work on a nearby ranch, but have been dropped off short of their destination by a bus-driver. It is obvious that Lennie is a half-wit, and George makes him get rid of a dead mouse he has been petting in his pocket.

Before the two men settle down to share a can of beans for supper, George gives Lennie strict instructions not to say anything when they meet the boss of the ranch the next day, because, 'If he finds out what a crazy bastard you are, we won't get no job', and makes Lennie throw the dead mouse away when he secretly goes to retrieve it. It emerges that in Weed, where they were previously working, Lennie stroked the material of a girl's dress, frightening her and giving rise to a rape charge. The two men had to hide in an irrigation ditch and flee the town. George gets angry with Lennie—'You crazy son-of-a-bitch. You keep me in hot water all the time'—but then relents, and as the sun sets, tells Lennie a story they have obviously been through many times before; Lennie almost knows it off by heart, but demands to hear it again from George. It is their dream, about how they are going to buy a few acres of land, raise their own animals, and live an independent and happy existence. They will have rabbits on the farm, and Lennie will be allowed to tend these and all the other animals. Comforted by the story of their dream, they go to sleep.

COMMENTARY: In this opening section of the novel Steinbeck displays his mastery of two different styles. The opening paragraph is powerful and evocative descriptive writing, concentrating on the simple colours seen in the landscape (green, yellow, gold, and white), and its inhabitants; no less than five types of animal (lizard, racoon, rabbit, dog, and deer) are mentioned in what is a very short paragraph. Simple though the description is, it is also detailed; it is not the leaves that are green, but the 'lower leaf junctures', and Steinbeck has time to notice that the deer tracks are 'split-wedge'. The other style at which Steinbeck excels is that of direct speech. His spellings suggest vividly the accents and intonations of his speakers, and each is characterised by his style of speech. Both are uneducated, but both reveal their natures by their manner of speech. George's is fast-flowing, its occasionally jerky rhythm suggesting a quick and active mind, always questioning, whilst Lennie's simple-mindedness is suggested by the shortness of his sentences, and his frequent pauses and repetitions, as with, 'I remember that ... but ... what'd we do then? I remember some girls come by and you says ... you says ...' Lenny is almost an animal—huge, simple, essentially well-meaning but liable to be frightened into doing violent things—and Steinbeck makes this point by association; he does not tell the reader directly that Lennie is like this, but instead describes Lennie in terms that are derived from the appearance and nature of animals. The reader is thus conditioned to think of Lennie as an animal. His legs and feet are described as being like those of a bear, his hand like a 'paw', and he is also compared to a horse, a carp, and a terrier dog. The last image suggests the master–slave relationship between George and Lennie, but is perhaps the least successful in this opening section, as it denies the concept of great size that has hitherto been associated with Lennie. Events in this section also foreshadow the ending of the novel. Lennie has been frightened into clinging on to a girl's dress in Weed, with disastrous consequences, and kills mice and small animals because he does not realise his own strength. Some critics have said that this knowledge makes it so clear what will happen at the end of the book that it removes all suspense from the novel, and is therefore a rather clumsy attempt to prepare the reader for what is to come. This allegation is dealt with more fully in Section 3. The opening of the novel also introduces the reader to George and Lennie's dream of a small farm, something which is central to the whole novel. A final point that is worth noting is the manner in which Steinbeck creates an atmosphere by producing carefully selected details of the natural environment. Warm colours and soft sounds combine in the description to give the reader a feeling of peace and contentment. When at the end of the novel, Steinbeck wishes to suggest a harsher and more cruel world, he alters only one detail from the opening description; the water-snake which was swimming peacefully in the pool at the start of the novel is still there at the end, but this time is plucked from the water and savagely eaten by a heron. This one alteration is sufficient to change the whole mood of the description, and prepares us for the shooting of Lennie by George, just as the earlier description prepared us for the peace and contentment that George feels as he contemplates sleeping under the stars.

NOTES AND GLOSSARY:

Soledad:	a small town on the Salinas River
Salinas River:	this flows through Southern California, one of the richest agricultural regions in the United States
Gabilan Mountains:	a small range of mountains overlooking Soledad
'coons:	racoons. A small, grey, furry animal, carnivorous and related to the bear family
split-wedge:	deer tracks are roughly triangular in shape, with a split up what would be the base of the triangle
jungle-up:	American slang, meaning to make camp or spend the night somewhere
stilted heron:	the heron is a large wading bird often found near shallow water or streams. Its long legs can make it appear as if it is walking on stilts, and it can appear very cumbersome when it launches itself into flight
pendula:	rarely used plural of pendulum, meaning a heavy weight on the end of a long piece of material that causes it to swing backwards and forwards
gonna:	going to
tha's:	that's
kinda:	kind of
oughta:	ought to
of rode clear:	have ridden clear
Jes' a little stretch:	just a short distance
ya:	you
awready:	already
gotta:	got to

jus':	just
spen':	spend
'em:	them
Murray and Ready's:	one of the projects in President Roosevelt's 'New Deal' was the setting-up of agencies, such as Murray and Ready's, which could direct agricultural and other workers to areas where there was employment
work cards:	Their new employer would require to see evidence that George and Lennie were the people he was expecting from Murray and Ready's before he took them on; work cards provided this evidence
musta:	must have
outa:	out of
on'y:	only
pet it:	stroke it, caress it
Weed:	an inland town in California, on the border with Oregon
that's swell:	that's good, that's right
fear ya:	for fear that you
run us outa Weed:	chased us out of Weed, drove us away
you on my tail:	you following me around, dependent on me
to-morra:	tomorrow
thrashin' machines:	machines which separate out the grain in a corn crop
bucking grain bags, bustin' a gut:	lifting and carrying heavy bags of grain, working very hard
gi'me:	give me
you ain't puttin' nothing over:	you're not hiding anything from me, you are not deceiving me
sock you:	hit you
terrier:	a small hunting dog
blubberin':	crying, in tears
ever':	every
bindle:	a bundle of clothes and cooking utensils, made portable by wrapping blankets round the outside
bucks:	American dollars
cat-house:	brothel
pool:	a game similar to billiards, and played on the same table, where balls have to be potted in a set order
shoot pool:	play pool
hot water:	trouble
I go nuts:	I go mad

coyote:	a prairie wolf
work up a stake:	earn and save up some money
blow their stake:	spend the money they have saved; the phrase implies that the money is spent on something worthless
poundin' their tail:	working very hard, up to breaking point
blowin' in our jack:	wasting our money
live off the fatta the lan':	live off the fat of the land; live in luxury
brush:	scrub-land, wild vegetation
Sacramento:	a large town in California, north-east of San Francisco

---

Section 2. Pages 20–37: *'The bunk-house was a long, rectangular building.'*

SUMMARY: George and Lennie are shown the bunk-house by Candy, the old man who cleans out the farm buildings. George is worried in case the previous occupant of his bunk has left it infested with lice, but is reassured by Candy. They meet the boss of the ranch, quite a reasonable man whose only weakness seems to be that when he is in a bad mood he loses his temper with the negro who runs the farm stable. He is suspicious of George and Lennie, but is eventually satisfied that they will do good work for him. Curley, the boss's son, comes into the bunk-house, and almost immediately starts an argument with Lennie; Curley is an ex-lightweight boxer who is always picking fights with people, and, to make him even more nervous, he has just married a young girl who appears to want to be unfaithful to him. George is convinced that there will be trouble between Lennie and Curley; he warns Lennie, and reminds him of where they are to meet if Lennie does get into any trouble. Curley's wife comes into the bunk-house, saying she is looking for Curley, and Lennie is fascinated by her. Then George and Lennie meet Slim, the 'jerk-line skinner' (see glossary), a man of great dignity and natural authority, and Carlson, a ranch-hand. Carlson reveals that Slim's dog had puppies the previous day, and suggests that one of the puppies be given to Candy, so that his old dog, which stinks and is senile, can be shot. Curley comes into the bunk-house again, and George is even more convinced that there will be trouble.

COMMENTARY: The main function of this section is to introduce the characters at the ranch, and prepare the reader even more fully for the end of the novel. The reader is left in no doubt that Lennie will somehow become involved with Curley and his wife. Slim is shown as a natural leader, and Carlson as a brutal, superficial man. Perhaps most interesting is Candy. It is typical of Steinbeck to characterise Candy through his dog; like its owner, it is physically decayed and hopeless, with nothing to look forward to except death. The portrait of Candy shows Steinbeck's sympathy for the underprivileged and the crippled. The cleanliness of George is emphasised, both physically (by his examination of the bunk for lice) and mentally (by his revulsion at hearing that Curley has vaseline in his glove). Steinbeck's gift for unusual but effective descriptive images is shown when he talks of the girl's hair, 'in little rolled clusters, like sausages'.

NOTES AND GLOSSARY:

burlap ticking:	coarse cloth, probably canvas, covering the bedding on the bunk
vials:	glass jars or bottles
roaches:	cockroaches
pants rabbits:	lice, fleas
swamper:	a cleaner; the word implies a menial or degrading job
grey-backs:	lice
bugs:	lice
quit:	left, dismissed himself
ta:	to
set:	sat
gimme my time:	give me the money due to me for the hours I have worked
tick:	mattress cover
bindle:	bundle of blankets
burned:	angry
stable buck:	the negro ('buck') who looks after the stables
brang:	brought
little skinner ... took after the nigger:	the driver of a small mule team took a dislike to the negro, and fought him
poop:	energy
stetson:	a large type of hat
a bum steer:	false or misleading information
short two buckers:	short of two loaders
rassel grain-bags:	load bags of grain
put up:	lift unaided
what you sellin'?:	what's your interest in this?
buck:	load
cesspool:	a pit for solid sewage waste
flapper:	mouth

nosey:	over-interested in the affairs of other people
ast:	ask
set:	sit
awright:	all right
old man:	slang for father
s'pose:	suppose
what the hell's he got on his shoulder?:	a reference to the phrase 'having a chip on your shoulder', meaning to be full of resentment and insecurity
handy:	a good fighter
the ring:	the boxing ring
take after:	argue with
scraps:	fights
punk:	American slang for a worthless person
licks:	beats, wins
game:	courageous, brave
oughtta:	ought to
gang up on:	join up together so as to outnumber and fight someone
slough:	literally, to cast off or shed, but in this context implying doing something unpleasant
canned:	sacked, dismissed
vaseline:	petroleum jelly, used as an ointment. The implication is sexual: Curley is keeping his hand soft for caressing his wife
Purty?:	Pretty?
she got the eye:	she is a flirt, she encourages men
pants is full of ants:	he is restless, ill-at-ease
jerkline skinner:	the jerkline is a single rein that runs to the lead animal in a team of mules or horses. A 'jerkline skinner' is a driver who can control the team by use of this one rein
tart:	a loose, flirtatious woman, a woman of low morals
solitaire:	a card game for one person, akin to the game of patience
set-up:	good environment
feelin' you out:	testing you
sock:	hit, punch
tangles:	picks a fight
to plug himself up for a fighter:	to get a good name for himself as a fighter, to earn a reputation
trace:	harness

let 'im have it:	hit him very hard
mules:	slippers without heels
bridled:	reacted, showed she was aware of what was happening
she's sure hidin' it:	an ironical remark. The girl is certainly not hiding her good looks
jail-bait:	the kind of girl who would get a man sent to prison; someone who can only bring harm to a man
take the rap:	take the blame
eatin' raw eggs:	George thinks Curley may be having to take rather extravagant measures to keep up his virility, in order to satisfy his wife
two bits:	a quarter, or twenty-five cents in American money
in the poke:	saved up
pan gold:	to wash through sand and soil in order to find gold
a pocket:	a rich vein of gold
the wheeler's butt:	the flank of the lead animal, the rear quarter
bright:	intelligent, clever
slang:	gave birth to
in heat:	ready for mating

Section 3. Pages 37–61: '*Although there was an evening brightness showing through . . .*'

SUMMARY: It is evening in the bunk house; Slim has given a puppy to Lennie, and he and George talk. George feels able to tell Slim why it is that he looks after Lennie, and to tell him how it was that they came to be thrown out of Weed: Lennie stroked the material of a girl's dress, and hung on in panic when she began to scream. She accused Lennie of rape, and they had to hide all day in an irrigation ditch to escape capture. Lennie tries to take his puppy to bed with him, but is stopped by George. Carlson cannot stand the smell of Candy's old dog, and asks Slim to give Candy one of his pups so that the old dog can be shot. The decision is postponed briefly when a young ranch-hand shows Slim a letter written in one of the western magazines that the hands love to read; it was written by a man who used to work at the ranch. Unwillingly, Candy lets Carlson take away his old dog to be shot, and is deeply upset. George and Whit, a ranch-hand, talk about Susy's, a local brothel where the men go on Saturday nights, and discuss Curley's wife. As they finish, Curley bursts in, and notices Slim is not there; he rushes out, thinking he is with his wife. Then Lennie comes in, and he and George start dreaming out loud about the little farm they are going to get. Candy listens, and suddenly asks if he can join them—he has three hundred and fifty dollars saved up. Then their dream is broken up by the arrival of Slim and Curley, with Slim furious at having been wrongly accused by Curley. Curley turns on Lennie, and attacks him viciously. Responding to George's orders, Lennie grabs Curley's hand and crushes it. Curley is rushed to hospital, but not before Slim has made him promise to say that his hand was caught in a machine, thus diverting any blame from Lennie.

COMMENTARY: This section contains the first major climax of the novel, the culmination of the tension that has been brewing between Curley and Lennie. The final climax of the novel is also foreshadowed, with the old dog being shot by the same Luger that will kill Lennie, and the story of the girl's red dress in Weed and Lennie dumbly crushing Curley's hand giving a hint as to what will happen in the stable with Curley's wife. The dream of Lennie and George is also put into perspective, and its impossibility emphasised. Just when George, Lennie, and Candy have convinced themselves that they really will get the little farm, there is a savage injection of real life into their world, with Curley's unprovoked attack on Lennie and its consequences showing the reader that the real world is much crueller and harsher than the one envisaged by the dreamers. The dream is not totally shattered by this incident (it is salvaged temporarily by Slim), but the reader is prepared for its final dissolution in the final section of the novel. The reader is also given an insight into the nature of George (Slim's description of him as a 'smart little guy' sums him up), and his reasons for staying with Lennie.

George admits that being near to Lennie gives him a feeling of superiority, although he has now stopped playing cruel tricks on Lennie to show off his command over him. Loneliness is emphasised as a major theme in this section. It is another reason why George stays with Lennie, it crops up in the way Slim describes a ranch-hand's life, and it is ever-present in Candy's life. The excitement caused by the ex-worker's letter to the western magazine shows that George and Lennie are not the only people who exist on dreams. The ranch-hands scoff at these magazines, but secretly believe in the stories they contain, and thus nourish themselves by dreams of what their life might be like, based on the romantic and exciting characters in the pulp magazines. The significance of light in Steinbeck's descriptions is also emphasised. Much of the atmosphere of the discussion between Slim and George at the start of the novel derives from the pool of light that the shaded lamp throws into the bunk-house. The delicacy with which Steinbeck handles the talk about brothels, whores, and venereal disease should also be noted. It could easily become obscene, coarse, and revolting, but under Steinbeck's hand it emerges as natural, a normal part of a man's life, and almost healthy.

NOTES AND GLOSSARY:

horse-shoe game: a game where horseshoes are thrown at an upright post set in the ground, with the object of encircling it

would of: would have

if it don't take no figuring: if it doesn't require any thought

string along: keep company together

cuckoo: a 'crazy' person, an idiot

fifty and found: fifty dollars a week, plus board and lodging

outa: out of

Auburn: a Californian town north-east of Sacramento

couda: could have

people: family

fence picket: a fence post

scairt: scared

rabbits: either rushes in, or talks volubly; both meanings are possible

scrammed: ran, fled

'um: him

jes': just

slug: drink

gut ache: stomach ache

knowed: knew

pitch shoes: throw horseshoes

Airedale: a rough-coated terrier, not normally associated with shepherding

pulp magazine: a 'trash' magazine printed on cheap, coarse, 'pulp' paper.

whing-ding: colloquial expression, signifying approval

dime: ten cents, the price of the magazine

books: he means magazines

Luger: a famous German make of pistol; it is this pistol that George will steal in order to shoot Lennie

tomorra: tomorrow

euchre: card game for two or four people

without turning his hand: without doing any work

roll up a stake: save up some money

looloo
presumably derived from the name Lulu, and meaning worth looking at, a loose woman

yella-jackets:
wasps (insects which sting!)

all set on the trigger: poised to get somebody into trouble

idears:
ideas

two and a half:
two and a half dollars

shot:
drink of whisky

flop:
sexual intercourse with one of the girls

joint:
place, establishment

kewpie doll lamp:
a lamp with a doll of a young child or an infant as its base

phonograph:
gramophone

clean:
free from syphilis or venereal disease

getting burned:
getting infected with venereal disease

bow-legged:
a reference to people who have been infected with venereal disease

three bucks a crack: three dollars a time for sexual intercourse

goo-goos:
there are three possible meanings for this phrase. It could mean 'do-gooders' or reformers, cheap whores, or negroes

spoilin':
ready for, wanting a fight

Golden Gloves:
an amateur boxing tournament, begun in 1928; the winner was awarded a gold medal

set him back:
cost him

hoosegow:
prison, jail

San Quentin:
one of the most notorious of American prisons, situated in California

alfalfa:
lucerne, a crop grown for feeding cattle

smoke-house:
a room or building that could be filled with dense smoke for the purpose of curing fish or meat

kin's:
kinds of

Jap cook:
a Japanese cook; quite common at the time on ranches, as they were relatively cheap labour, but obviously not appreciated!

does ... litter:
the female rabbits (does) would breed rapidly

flat bust:
bankrupt, penniless

kick off:
die

on the county:
on charity relief payments

little chicken stuff: odd jobs, trivial tasks

swing her:
persuade her, or get the job done

squack:
no meaning as such; the sound of the word emphasises the immediacy and certainty of the decision

ast: asked
yella as a frog belly: a coward
welter: welterweight, a weight in boxing
leggo: let go
candy-wagon: a trap or buggy; carriage used for transporting people, and not for farm-work
lit intil: attacked

Section 4. Pages 61–75: *'Crooks, the negro stable buck, had his bunk in the harness-room.'*

SUMMARY: Lennie walks into Crooks's room, and his simplicity disarms Crooks's initial hostility. Lennie reveals the plan to buy a small farm, and the cynical Crooks teases Lennie about what will happen if George does not come back from town, where he has gone with the other hands. Crooks is frightened by Lennie's response, and reveals how lonely he is. Candy enters the room (it is the first time he has set foot in there in all the time that he and Crooks have been working on the ranch), and talks about the farm he is going to move to with George and Lennie. Crooks pours scorn on the idea, but seems to be on the verge of being won round, and even asks if he can come to work on the farm when it is bought. He is interrupted by Curley's wife. The men in the room are upset and nervous in her presence, and she asks (without receiving a true answer) how it was that Curley's hand came to be crushed. She talks about her loneliness, and finally goads Candy into telling her to get out. Crooks even seems prepared to stand up to her, but she silences him immediately by threatening to accuse him of raping her, a charge which would result in his being hanged. She leaves, but not before she has confessed to hating Curley. George comes to look for Lennie, and the white men leave Crooks's room; Candy withdraws his request to come and work with George, Lennie, and Candy. He too has been drawn into the dream, but his treatment at the hands of Curley's wife has brought him back to reality, and shown him the impossibility of achieving it.

COMMENTARY: This section revolves round Crooks, and his pathetic search for dignity and self-respect in a world which will allow the negro neither. Crooks is a cripple, but obviously intelligent, yet he has no defence against even so worthless a person as Curley's wife; the girl can reduce him to a cringing nonentity with no trouble at all. Yet in this section the reader can also generate some sympathy for the girl. She too is lonely, and has her dream, the pathetic one of joining a travelling show or making her name in the movie industry. Again in this section the dream is shattered. The memory of it allows Candy and Crooks to stand up against the girl for a brief while, but it is short-lived, and the realities of life rapidly emerge again to take over. The function of this section is to elaborate on the themes of loneliness, and rejected people like Candy and Crooks. It also provides a relative lull in the story before the major climaxes of the last two sections.

NOTES AND GLOSSARY:

hame: part of the collar of a horse or mule, through which the reins pass

California civil code for 1905: an out-dated book of laws

dirty books: obscene, pornographic books

set: sit

crazy as a wedge: crazy, mad

nail-keg: a small barrel for holding nails and screws

I ain't a southern negro: Southern negroes were historically and traditionally more enslaved and subservient than those in the north of the United States

blabbin': telling other people

screwy: mad, incomprehensible

took a powder: went away

booby hatch: lunatic asylum

rummy: a card game

nuts: mad, insane

measure by: judge by

wun't: wouldn't

do': don't

blackjack: a card game

ast: ask

alla: all of the

two-by-four: small

baloney: rubbish

bindle bums: travelling tramps

pitchers: pictures, movies

som'pin: something

bindle stiffs: idiots, worthless people

dum-dum: idiot, half-wit

floosy idears: wrong ideas. A floosy is a girl of loose morals

two shots of corn: two drinks of whisky

go along an' roll your hoop: go away and play childish games

doped out: worked out, thought out

Section 5. Pages 75–88: '*One end of the great barn was piled high with new hay . . .*'

SUMMARY: Lennie is in the barn, stroking his puppy; he has killed it accidentally. Outside in the yard the men are holding a horse-shoe game tournament. Curley's wife comes, bored and restless. Despite Lennie's opposition (he remembers George's advice to him), she insists on sitting beside him and talking about her life. She thinks she could have joined a travelling show when she was fifteen, and become an actress. She remembers a man she met at a dance who promised to introduce her to the movies and make her star material, but she never received the letter he promised to write. Convinced that her mother stole it, she married Curley out of spite, and to get away from home. Lennie carries on thinking about the rabbits. She gets Lennie to admit that he likes stroking soft things, and makes him stroke her hair. He strokes too hard and she cries out, frightening Lennie and making him cling on to her. When she will not stop screaming, Lennie shakes her, and accidentally breaks her neck. He remembers George's instructions to make for the brush if he gets into trouble, and creeps away. Candy discovers the body, and brings George to see it, guessing the murderer must be Lennie. George and Candy realise this is the end of their dream. George slips back to the bunk-house, so as not to be implicated in the murder. Candy tells the other hands about the body, and Slim pronounces that her neck has been broken, and suggests Lennie must be the murderer. They all set off to find Lennie, armed with shotguns; there seems little doubt that Curley will shoot to kill, although Carlson comes back to report that his pistol has been taken.

COMMENTARY: There is an air of inevitability about this section as it hurries towards its terrible climax, partly because there are fewer descriptive passages and a more terse style, and partly because the reader has been prepared for something like the death of Curley's wife right from the start of the novel. Nevertheless, the opening description of the barn is quite full, and again relies heavily on a description of light and shade. There are two strong ironies in the section. The first is that in their conversation before the killing, Curley's wife and Lennie reveal how similar they are, at least in one respect; they both have impossible dreams, he of his farm and she of a career in Hollywood, that are destined never to be realised. Both will shortly be dead. The second irony concerns Carlson's Luger. We find out later that it has been taken by George, in case he finds he has to kill Lennie as an act of mercy. But the act of taking the gun insures that Lennie will be shot, because the hunters think Lennie has it, and is dangerous; thus they will not agree to capture him, and are only concerned to shoot him. George's precautionary measure ensures the death of Lennie. The actual moment of the girl's death is superbly understated, 'And then she was still, for Lennie had broken her neck', but criticisms have been made of another paragraph, when Steinbeck writes:

> As happens sometimes, a moment settled and hovered and remained for much more than a moment. And sound stopped and movement stopped for much, much more than a moment.

Some critics have felt that this is unduly poetic, a richly literary piece of writing that sits at odds with the more objective and impersonal style that Steinbeck uses elsewhere. It could also be argued that it is highly effective, capturing the stillness of this terrible moment in its entirety.

NOTES AND GLOSSARY:

fin's:	finds
tenement:	tournament
mutt:	a mongrel
fulla:	full of
movies:	moving pictures, the cinema
Hollywood:	the centre of the American motion picture industry
previews:	screenings of films before they are generally available to the public
a natural:	actress, or star
made a ringer:	threw the horseshoe on to the peg
sof':	soft
wisht:	wish
muss it up:	mess it up, make it untidy
oughten':	ought not to
usta:	used to
would of went:	could have gone

Section 6. Pages 88-95: *'The deep green pool of the Salinas River was still . . .'*

SUMMARY: Lennie waits for George in the clearing by the pool. He sees a vision of his Aunt Clara, which reprimands him. It is then replaced by a vision of a giant rabbit that tells Lennie George will now leave him, after what he has done. Lennie is crying out for George when he appears from the brush. George talks quietly and apparently calmly to Lennie, and repeats the old tales in a wooden voice, without emphasis.

The sounds of the hunters draw nearer. George tells Lennie to look away from him, across the river, to where he will almost be able to see the farm they will buy. He shoots the unsuspecting Lennie in the back of the head with Carlson's Luger. Curley, Carlson, Slim and the others arrive, drawn by the shot. Only Slim understands what is going through George's mind, and the two leave the others and go off down the highway for a drink.

COMMENTARY: It has been said this last section is an anti-climax; that there is no reason why Lennie could not have been captured and handed over to the authorities; that Steinbeck is too sentimental; and that the shooting of Lennie is simply too neat and convenient an ending to be convincing. Whatever the truth of the matter (and this problem is discussed in Part 3), the ending as it stands is a fine and dramatic piece of writing, and in the context of the novel can seem as inevitable as did the trouble between Lennie, Curley, and the girl. It has also been argued that there is no reason why the dream had to be shattered, as it was perfectly reasonable and possible for George, Lennie, and Candy to get the farm of their dreams. Critics who argue this overlook one of the main themes of the novel, that people need dreams to see them through their dull and often harsh lives, but that these dreams rarely if ever achieve fruition. There might appear to be a contrast in this section between the peace and beauty of the natural surroundings, and the harshness of Lennie's death, but Steinbeck is careful to include his heron 'lancing down' to kill the water-snake to show the reader that peace and violence can co-exist in nature. To the very end of the novel Steinbeck continues to use certain descriptive techniques, notably describing Lennie in terms of animals, and using light as a major element in his descriptive passages. One of the finest images in the whole novel is that of the sun blazing on the Gabilan Mountains, just as George prepares to kill Lennie.

NOTES AND GLOSSARY:

hern: heron

bull's-eye glasses: spectacles with almost white glass and a darker centre

gingham: dyed cotton or linen, with a simple check pattern

stew the b'Jesus outa George: make life difficult for George

jack you outa the sewer: keep you out of trouble

fambly: family

snapped off the safety: released the safety-catch, so the gun was ready to fire

eatin': worrying

Part 3

Commentary

The title

The title of the novel is taken from the poem 'To a Mouse' by the Scottish poet Robert Burns (1759–96):

> *The best laid schemes o' mice and men*
> *Gang aft agley*
> *And leave us nought but grief and pain*
> *For promised joy.*

Burns is saying that men's dreams and plans often go wrong, and bring trouble and heartache instead of joy. This, of course, is what happens to the plans of George and Lennie. Burns brings mice into his poem to emphasise the smallness and helplessness of man when pitted against the forces of fate and destiny, and this same feeling is evident in Steinbeck's novels. Right from the start of the novel, there is an awareness that what George and Lennie are discussing is an impossible dream, destined to be thwarted and shattered by inevitable forces over which they have no control. There is no particular connection between Burns's mention of mice and Lennie's fondness for them.

Plot and structure

Some critical works on *Of Mice and Men* spend a considerable amount of time discussing whether the book is a long short-story, a short long story, a novel, or a *novella* (a short novel). Much of this discussion is fruitless, as it is relatively unimportant what name is given to the book provided that its basic structure is understood. In essence the book is a short novel, and the term *novella* can be used of it.

The basic structure of the novel is simple. There are six sections with all except the first and last centred on the bunk-house and the ranch. These sections are clearly distinguished from each other in setting and content, and it might be asked why Steinbeck did not do the obvious thing, and make each of these sections a separate chapter. One answer is that there is no rule or regulation that demands an author should have chapters in his work, and that its being a convention of prose fiction writing is no good reason why we should demand its appearance in *Of Mice and Men*; if the novel is ever to make any advances, writers must feel free to decide their own structure. Another reason, and the one which probably influenced Steinbeck, is that breaking up the story into chapters would inevitably force a break of concentration upon the reader. *Of Mice and Men* is a tightly structured book, economically written and fast-moving, and it could be argued that splitting it up into chapters could make it less fluent, and destroy the build-up of atmosphere. There is an inevitability about the story, a feeling that the characters are implacably set on the road to a disaster, and separate chapters might break up and destroy this feeling. Certainly the atmosphere of inevitability is helped by the cyclical nature of the story, whereby the last section returns to the setting used for the first. It is as if George and Lennie have set out on a journey which has led nowhere, only back to where they started from, and that this being the case, the destruction of their relationship is the only way left. They have tried to move and alter, but the limitations of Lennie have brought them back to their starting-point, and yet again reversed all their hopes and expectations. Aptly, the only course left to them is the final reversal, death for Lennie.

Steinbeck has been criticised for making the story too inevitable, and for being clumsy in dropping hints as to what the outcome of the book will be. The hints are certainly there in plenty: Lennie's killing of mice, the story of what happened in Weed, the fight with Curley, the killing of the puppy, the emphasis on his vast strength, the girl's interest in him, and George's oft-repeated assertions that the girl is 'jail-bait' and will bring trouble all seem to point to Lennie's eventual murder of the girl, and give rise to two criticisms. The first is that the reader loses all sense of suspense, and has the outcome of the story revealed to him at too early a stage. This criticism is not valid. It would be so if *Of Mice and Men* were a detective story, where the reader is not supposed to know the truth until almost the last page, but this is not the case. If anything, the book is a character study, and never intends to gain the reader's interest through the medium of suspense. Many works of literature do not bother to hide their ending. In particular, there can be few members of the audience who go to see a tragedy who can be in any doubt as to the eventual death of the tragic hero by about half-way through the play. The second criticism, that Steinbeck is clumsy in the preparation he gives the reader for the ending, is more difficult to dismiss. This view accepts that there is no harm in the reader guessing the ending of the novel, but complains that he is too aware of the manner in which he is being prepared. Good technique in a writer is when he can prepare the reader for what is to happen without the reader realising that his response is being manipulated; it has even been said that any technique which the reader is aware of is bad technique, in that the reader should only be aware of what is being said, not how it is being said. It is as if Steinbeck suddenly leaps out of the novel to give the reader a hearty nudge in the ribs to show him where he is going. With a problem like this, the critic can only suggest a variety of responses; in the event, it is the reader himself who must decide whether he finds this aspect of the plot annoying and clumsy, or valid in the context of the book as a whole.

The structure of the book is simple, yet skilful. The opening sequence, by the pool in the river, gives the reader a chance to get to know George and Lennie before they move into the slightly wider society of the ranch. Steinbeck introduces only a small number of characters, and two settings, thus keeping the structure and content of the book very straightforward. The story is unfolded chronologically with none of the moving backwards and forwards in time that is common in many modern novels. Simple though they may be, the plot and structure of *Of Mice and Men* should not be dismissed lightly; Steinbeck's technique may appear effortless, but this is a mark of his skill.

Themes

The themes of a work of literature are the particular ideas which an author examines in the course of a work, either to make a point or to enlarge the reader's understanding of them. Themes should not be confused with subject. The subject of *Of Mice and Men* is George and Lennie; its themes are ideas such as loneliness, dreams, and the working man, which are emphasised and brought to light by the way in which the author handles his subject.

The American Dream

One of Steinbeck's themes in *Of Mice and Men* is the dreams that people have. The main one, of course, is that of George and Lennie, so powerful that it later attracts Candy, and temporarily even the cynical Crooks. It is a very simple dream:

> 'Well, it's ten acres,' said George. 'Got a little win'mill. Got a little shack on it, an' a chicken run. Got a kitchen, orchard, cherries, apples, peaches, 'cots, nuts, got a few berries. They's a place for alfalfa and plenty water to flood it. They's a pig-pen ....'

It is also a dream that is shared by thousands of itinerant ranch-hands, few of whom have any hope of attaining it. Crooks sums this up:

'You're nuts.' Crooks was scornful. 'I see hunderds of men come by on the road an' on the ranches with their bindles on their back an' that same damn thing in their heads. Hunderds of them. They come, an' they quit an' go on; an' every damn one of 'em's got a little piece of land in his head . . . . . I read plenty of books out here. Nobody never gets to heaven, and nobody never gets no land. It's just in their head. They're all the time talkin' about it, but it's jus' in their head.'

George and Lennie are not the only people with a dream in the book. Curley's wife has one too, different in content from George and Lennie's, but serving the same purpose:

'Coulda been in the movies, an' had nice clothes—all of them nice clothes like they wear. An' I coulda sat in them big hotels, an' had pitchers took of me. When they had them previews I coulda went to them, an' spoke in the radio, an' it wouldn't cost me a cent because I was in the pitcher. An' all them nice clothes like they wear.'

Even the most ordinary ranch-hands read the pulp magazines, and dream that they might be like the heroes in the western stories that they contain.

Steinbeck shows that ordinary people need these dreams to survive. Often their lives are dull and unsatisfactory, and they are denied status, respect, and fulfilment by the way they live. They are caught in a trap, and there is no escape but for the fantasy world of the dream where an idea can be hatched and clung on to through the dark years, giving solace and comfort and the hope that, one day, the dream might come true.

Yet George's and Lennie's dream goes deeper even than this, right to the heart of a central concept in American thinking. For many years, America was a country with a frontier; early colonisation of the country took place on the eastern coast, and only gradually did the settlers spread until they finally reached the West Coast and the Pacific Ocean. Historians have suggested that for hundreds of years this concept of the frontier played a vital role in American thinking. People were conditioned to think of the frontier as a line beyond which civilisation ceased to exist. Beyond the frontier lay thousands of miles of land, there for the taking, and a life of excitement and adventure, where men could live free of the cares and burdens of urban or modern living. Above all, man beyond the frontier was free man, answerable only to himself. The frontier was probably never actually like this, but this did not stop it from becoming 'The American Dream'. It was a safety-valve, in that even though the vast majority of the population never took advantage of what the frontier lands offered, the thought that they could do so if they wanted was a comfort and solace to them. By 1900, there was no more frontier; the settlers had reached the ocean. American society had to come to terms with the fact that America was now a civilised, colonised country, but the way it did this was to perpetuate even more, in literature and in the cinema, the myth of the frontier. It is no accident that the heroes of American legend are the men of the frontier—Davy Crockett and Daniel Boone (legendary frontier fighters) and General Custer (another famous but ill-fated fighter against the Indians) and all the rest. It was as if the society needed this as assurance that man could still live free from care and close to nature, a truly independent animal and not merely as one of the cogs in a machine. Seen in this light, George's and Lennie's dream achieves even greater significance, and the popularity of it amongst ranch-hands in general is explained, for their dream is in essence a variation of the great American dream. Their ten-acre farm may not seem particularly close to the frontier, but it shares two major elements with it—closeness to nature and, above all, independence. George and Lennie will actually be able to harvest the crops they have planted, and be able to take time off to go to the carnival if they want to; they will be their own masters, answerable only to themselves.

All this might seem to make *Of Mice and Men* a particularly American novel, limited in its relevance to the inhabitants of other countries, but this is not so. The dream of Lennie and George is couched in peculiarly American terms, but its spirit is universal. The little child who dreams of driving a railway-engine or being a jet-pilot, the poor peasant who dreams of the extra cow or pig that will put him above the starvation level, the ageing middle-class businessman who dreams of retirement and a house by the sea, all these in essence share the same dream of a life that will combine a feeling of freedom with personal fulfilment. George's and Lennie's dream is couched in American terms, but it speaks clearly to all those who have felt hemmed-in and constricted by society.

Yet Steinbeck does more than present the dream; he shows it smashed and disintegrated. The fact that it is not a great dream that is being destroyed, but merely a very humble one of ten acres and a few animals, makes it all the more tragic. There is irony in the fact that the very freedom George and Lennie crave is in part responsible for Lennie's death; in a less free society, Lennie would not have been allowed to roam with George, but would have been locked up in an asylum from the start, or at the least a special school. It is the freedom that George and Lennie have that lets Lennie do that for which he must be killed. It is equally true to say that all is not lost at the end of the novel. Throughout its length the farm they will buy has been seen as a symbol of a certain set of values, a pure, clean, and independent way of living. George's decision to shoot Lennie springs from these same values, odd though it may sound to describe such a decision as pure and clean. Were Lennie to be captured, he would either be brutally killed, or locked up. As it is, Lennie dies painlessly, in a state of happiness, at the hands of the only other human who means anything to him. He dies free, and in the midst of nature, as perhaps he might have died had they ever bought the farm. Another thing the farm has stood for is consideration for other people. On it, there was to be no bullying into work, no labouring up to the point of exhaustion. George shoots Lennie because of consideration for him. As Slim says, 'A guy got to sometimes', and instant death at George's hands is the kindest thing that can happen to Lennie after what he has done.

As Steinbeck portrays it, the dream appears in many lights; at various times it appears as intensely moving, pathetic, a practical possibility, and pure wishful thinking. The one thing Steinbeck carefully avoids doing is giving a neat answer to the problems it poses. The reader is never told in clear and unequivocal terms that the dream is a bad thing, or a good thing. It simply exists, and, in Steinbeck's version, will always continue to do so whilst men are denied the things that would make their lives truly fulfilling. To claim it as a good or bad thing would be as senseless as complaining about the heron that kills the water-snake at the end of the book. Both are parts of life and nature, so inevitable that human comment on them is almost superfluous.

This raises the question whether *Of Mice and Men* is a pessimistic book. Certainly, its ending is unhappy, at least in the conventional sense of the word, but there is a great deal more than pessimism in it. There is, for instance, George's care for Lennie and his compassion, Lennie's unaffected love for George, and Slim's natural dignity. Steinbeck does seem to be saying that dreams like that of Lennie and George will never be realised, but he also says that in the pursuit of these dreams people can generate feelings and ideas that are as pure and noble as the ideals of the dream itself. One of the key features of *Of Mice and Men* is balance, between the good and the bad, the unhappy and the unhappy. If Steinbeck refuses to come down in favour of one side or the other, it is not because he is frightened or confused, but because he sees life as neither black nor white, but balanced in between—a blend of both colours, with neither dominating.

Loneliness

Loneliness is another theme in *Of Mice and Men*. Of all the characters, George is the one who expresses this theme most powerfully:

'Guys like us, that work on ranches, are the loneliest guys in the world. They got no family. They don't belong no place. They come to a ranch an' work up a stake and then they go inta town and blow their stake, and the first thing you know they're poundin' their tail on some other ranch. They ain't got nothing to look ahead to.'

The point that George is making is that he and Lennie have each other, and can thus stave off the pangs of loneliness that afflict all other ranch-hands. However, it is not merely the ranch-hands who are lonely in *Of Mice and Men*. Curley's wife says to Lennie:

'Why can't I talk to you? I never get to talk to nobody. I get awful lonely.'

and later, 'her words tumbled out in a passion of communication, as though she hurried before her listener could be taken away.' It is her loneliness that leads to her death. Candy and Crooks are examples of a different kind of loneliness, that of the cripple and the misfit. Candy is lonely because he is old, past his prime, and has no one to care for him, and because he has lost a hand. Crooks is lonely because society shuns a cripple and a negro, counting for nothing the intelligence that lies just beneath his skin and his deformity. Loneliness affects these two men in different ways. It makes Candy turn to his dog, until even that is taken away from him, and Crooks is forced behind a defensive barrier of cynicism and dull obedience, his brain seething all the while.

Steinbeck is not an intellectual. He puts forward no great theories about loneliness, and is content merely to state and illustrate its presence. The overriding feature that emerges from his vision of loneliness is the feeling of compassion and sympathy for those so afflicted by it. If he does make a point, it is that warmth and human companionship are as vital to a human being as food and water.

Protest

Of Mice and Men is not a political novel, nor one which sets out to castigate American society. The ranch-hands get their fifty dollars a month and keep, seem to eat well, and have a reasonable boss. Yet it is still possible to see *Of Mice and Men* as a protest novel, with its voice directed in particular against three ills: racial discrimination, the treatment of old age, and the plight of the farm-worker who never reaps what he sows.

Crooks obviously illustrates one aspect of racial prejudice. He reads books, is intelligent, and, like any human being, needs warmth and companionship. Yet he is denied these, not because of any inherent fault, but because he is a negro. He sums up his situation in his own words:

> Crooks said gently: 'Maybe you can see now. You got George. You *know* he's goin' to come back. S'pose you didn't have nobody. S'pose you couldn't go into the bunk-house and play rummy 'cause you was black. How'd you like that? S'pose you had to sit out here an' read books. Sure you could play horseshoes till it got dark, but then you got to read books. Books ain't no good. A guy needs somebody—to be near him.' He whined: 'A guy goes nuts if he ain't got nobody. Don't make no difference who the guy is, long's he's with you. I tell ya,' he cried, 'I tell ya a guy gets too lonely an' he gets sick.'

Superficially this passage is a complaint against the racial prejudice that denies Crooks solace and companionship. It undoubtedly has this function, but it must also be seen in a wider context as even more a part of a theme that has already been discussed, that of loneliness. It is loneliness that is the root of Crooks's complaint. In his case, it is loneliness brought about by racial prejudice, but the centre of attention is the illness itself, not its cause. Racial prejudice and discrimination thus appear in *Of Mice and Men*, but not as a theme in their own right. They are simply part of the larger tapestry of the theme of loneliness.

Much the same could be said about the apparent theme of how old people are treated. The vehicle for this idea is Candy. He is old and tired, waiting to be thrown on the scrap-heap when he can no longer work, like a soulless machine that has served its purpose. He clutches at George's dream as the only escape from his fate. One passage in particular sums up the cruelty of what is going to happen to him:

> 'You see what they done to my dog tonight? They says he wasn't no good to himself nor nobody else. When they can me here I wisht somebody'd shoot me. But they won't do nothing like that. I won't have no place to go, an' I can't get no more jobs.'

Again, the complaint seems to be against the society which will discard an old man like this, after having used him for all his working life. But on closer examination, the real complaint is seen to be against loneliness; it is loneliness that turned Crooks into a cynical and bitter man, and it is loneliness—no 'folks' and no place to go—that haunts Candy.

There is a complaint against the cruelty of society, as there was a complaint about racial prejudice, but both are dominated by the greater theme of loneliness.

The third area of protest in the novel is not linked to loneliness. It is summed up when Candy says:

'I planted crops for damn near ever'body in this state, but they wasn't my crops, and when I harvested 'em, it wasn't none of my harvest.'

The farm-worker is closer to the land than anybody, closer even than the owner of the land. His sweat goes into the soil when the crops are sown and when they are harvested, but he cannot claim ownership from the land of what he has produced. This is Candy's complaint, and it is one of the oldest themes in literature; it would have been understood and recognised by William Langland (c. 1331–99?), the author of the fourteenth-century English poem *Piers Plowman* (c. 1376, but existing .in several versions.

The working man

It is rather difficult to decide whether the working man is a theme of *Of Mice and Men*, or simply a subject, but if it is a subject, it is one to which Steinbeck gives a great deal of prominence. The characters of the book are drawn from a quite narrow social range, with only the ranch boss coming from a higher social order, together with his son Curley. What Steinbeck does is to show us the working man in all his variations, revealing what a wide range of character and personality is to be found on a ranch among the hands. There is the quick-wittedness and loyalty of George, the slowness of Lennie; the natural dignity and leadership of Slim and the ingrowing, bitter cynicism of Crooks; the brutality of Carlson, the superficiality of Whit, and the sad fatalism of Candy. It has been said that Steinbeck is too interested in the misfits and the cripples, and that therefore his portrait is not an accurate one. However, this is a minor issue, the main one being the portrait of Slim. He is a 'princely' person, a natural leader, and a man possessed of immense dignity. In this portrait Steinbeck seems to be saying that natural leaders and men of authority will emerge in all ranks of society. It is clear that Slim, a 'jerk-line skinner', is also a man of great practical skill, and in many of Steinbeck's novels he seems to reserve his admiration for such men. There is certainly a tendency in Steinbeck's work to rate the man with practical skills above the man with intellectual ability. This is perhaps another very American feature in his work. The frontier man could build his own house, farm his own crops, deliver his own animals of their young, mend agricultural machinery, make his own cartridges, skin and cure animal hide, and brew his own drink, at least in legend, and thus do the jobs of a modern builder, farmer, veterinary surgeon, agricultural engineer, gunsmith, tanner, brewer, and carpenter—quite an overpowering list! The one thing that the old frontier heroes appeared to have done without was books, apart from an old copy of the Holy Bible. Steinbeck is therefore not unusual in the admiration he expresses for Slim, but is instead partaking of a tradition in American fiction.

Characterisation

General Points

Steinbeck is a very skilful creator of characters. His portraits are brief and economical, but also vivid and convincing. His technique is to give a brief preliminary description of the character, relying heavily on physical appearance, and then to let the character convey his own personality to the reader by means of what he does, but more significantly by his speech. Steinbeck does not take the reader inside the mind of his characters, and tell him what the character is thinking (a technique common in many modern novels); instead, he lets the character express his own fears, worries, and hopes, in one of two ways. George, Candy, and Crooks are all given speeches in which they confess their deepest feelings, as is Curley's wife when she confides in the unwilling Lennie. Curley, on the other hand, has no such speech; he is characterised by his actions, and by what other people (notably Candy and George) say about him. Carlson's attitude to Candy, Candy's dog, and Curley is enough to tell the reader all he needs to know about him. Slim is the character who receives the most complex treatment. He is a self-contained man, and so it would be unrealistic to give him a speech like George's or Candy's, expressing all his hopes and fears. We learn much about him from the other characters, none of whom mention him without respect and affection. Even the two most unlikely characters in the book, Crooks and Curley, appear to respect him. His speech is slow and measured in its rhythm, suggesting calmness and authority, and all his actions show a decisive and unquestioned authority. It is only with Slim that Steinbeck intervenes directly to tell the reader what he should think of him, perhaps an illustration of the special role which Steinbeck allots him in the novel.

Physical description, actions, and speech are therefore the major techniques used by Steinbeck in his portraits. One of the greatest achievements of the book is that the author can provide so many vivid portraits in only ninety or so pages. Some critics have complained that the portraits and the characters are almost too vivid, that a real ranch would contain more ordinary people, not the distinctive individuals with whom Steinbeck peoples the bunk-house. The conclusion drawn from this is that the characterisation is unrealistic. This is a difficult argument to support. The methods of characterisation sketched out above are essentially realistic. In real life, people form their judgements of other people on the basis of what they look like, what they do, and what they say, and in this respect Steinbeck is following the pattern of real life; a novelist who goes inside a character's head may produce a vivid picture, but it runs the risk of being an unrealistic one in that in real life people cannot go so deeply into the mind of a person. It should also be remembered that Steinbeck is almost certainly trying to make a point by presenting the characters he does, namely that people are rarely ordinary, in the sense of being unremarkable, but are all individuals with distinctive characters and problems of their own. In his portrait of Candy, Steinbeck may well be complaining that it is too easy to dismiss an old man as a worthless piece of human debris, and forget that underneath he is as human as anyone, with his own feelings and dignity. The best example of this is Lennie; on outward appearances he is a 'dum-dum', a half-wit, but as George knows, he is also an individual, a character, and a human being.

For convenience, it is necessary in this section to describe each character separately. This should not blind the reader to another area in which Steinbeck shows considerable skill, that of conveying the atmosphere and tensions that exist within a group situation. Thus Steinbeck can not only describe individuals vividly, but also their reaction when they are placed within a group, and the way that they relate to other people. This ability can be seen at its strongest in the section where Candy's dog is taken out to be shot. Each of the characters present tries to comfort Candy, each tries to stop listening for the fatal shot, and each feels a form of guilt at what is happening.

George

The first man was small and quick, dark of face, with restless eyes and sharp, strong features. Every part of him was defined: small, strong hands, slender arms, a thin and bony nose.

George and Slim are the heroes of *Of Mice and Men*. George is intelligent and quick-witted, in Slim's words 'a smart little guy'. There is a contradiction here which George himself points out.

'If I was bright, if I was even a little bit smart, I'd have my own little place, an' I'd be bringing in my own crops, 'stead of doin' all the work and not getting what comes up outa the ground.'

One answer to why George is just a ranch-hand is simply economic; he cannot buy his own ranch, and the world shown in *Of Mice and Men* is not one in which intelligence on its own can earn success. If it were, Crooks would have his own ranch as well, instead of being a mere stable buck. Another reason why George remains a ranch-hand is Lennie. If George is to look after Lennie, wandering around the ranches is probably the only way they can keep together. A long stay in any one area simply increases the chances of Lennie doing something wrong, and permanent employment would be too risky. This in turn raises the question of why George stays with Lennie; he tells him frequently about the freedom he could have if Lennie were not there with him, as frequently as he tells Lennie about the dream; Lennie knows both speeches off by heart.

George is a kind, soft-hearted person. The anger and sharpness that can be sometimes seen in him is not a reflection of his real temperament, but the result of the way he is forced to live, and the tensions that inevitably come with having to look after Lennie and get him out of trouble.

Undoubtedly George has come to like Lennie, and feels a sense of duty and responsibility towards him. But there is more to their partnership than this. Lennie needs George, and would be lost without him, but it is equally true to say that George needs Lennie. George is a thinker. All around him he sees the itinerant, nomadic farm workers, rootless and lonely, ineffective and lost. The companionship with Lennie is what staves off the horrors of loneliness. It does more than this; it gives George a sense of being different, not like all the thousands of ranch-hands. As Slim says, 'I hardly never seen two guys travel together', and their relationship makes George unusual, gives him distinction and even status. George and Lennie say it all themselves:

'We got a future. We got somebody to talk to that gives a damn about us. We don't have to sit in no bar-room blowin' in our jack jus' because we got no place else to go. If them other guys gets in jail they can rot for all anybody gives a damn. But not us.'

Lennie broke in. '*But not us! An' why? Because . . . because I got you to look after me, and you got me to look after you, and that's why.*' He laughed delightedly.

Certainly George looks after Lennie because he is a good, kind, loyal person, but he also does it because the relationship gives him something he desperately needs.

George is a good judge of other people's characters. He can sense that Curley and his wife will bring trouble, and that Slim is a man to be trusted. He is quiet, causing no trouble in the bunk-house, modest, and a good worker. He is clean-living, partly because he does not feel he can waste money in the pool-room and brothel if he is ever to buy the farm he covets, but partly also because of his temperament; he is appalled by Lennie drinking scummy water, and horrified that there might be lice in his bedding. He is a peaceful man, but cannot resist a certain delight in telling Lennie to 'get' Curley.

Some critics talk about George in terms of his capacity for moral growth, arguing that his relationship with Lennie matures him, forces him to think more, and increases his awareness of moral problems. It is certainly true that George does grow up in one sense; originally he played cruel tricks on Lennie, but stopped when he realised how childish and unthinking this was, and in his decision to shoot Lennie he finally takes full responsibility for the fate of another human being.

However, terms such as moral growth can be confusing and mis-leading, if only because they make a simple issue appear more complex than it actually is. There is no moral growth involved in George's decision to kill Lennie, at least in the sense of something new being added to his character. What does happen in the shooting is that a number of features which George has possessed all along are fused together, and seen for the first time acting as one, whereas before they have been seen separately. George is moral, as is seen by his distaste for brothels and his remark that 'That's dirty thing to tell around' when told about Curley's glove full of vaseline. It is his morality that tells him Lennie cannot be allowed to run away this time, for now he has actually murdered someone. George is full of compassion, and it is this that makes him prefer a clean death for Lennie, rather than a lynching or locking him up for life. George is a realist and knows the world, and so knows that society will not let Lennie get away this time. George is a responsible person; he brought Lennie to the farm, and so the responsibility for carrying out the punishment is also his. George has made sacrifices in order to look after Lennie. When he kills him, he makes the greatest sacrifice of all; Lennie dies with the words and expression of the dream on his lips and face, and when he dies, so does the dream, killed by the man who brought it into being. A point often missed in studying *Of Mice and Men* is the thoroughness with which Steinbeck prepares the reader for George's action in killing Lennie. It is often remarked that the reader is given plenty of clues as to what Lennie will eventually do, less so that all the clues are there as well to predict what George will do. George does not have to engage in any 'moral growth' in order to shoot Lennie; everything necessary for him to take this decision has been presented previously, in the early pages of the book. Indeed, moral destruction might be a better word for what happens to George. He is almost an empty shell when he leaves after the shooting with Slim, a man whose best characteristics have led only to his having to shoot the thing he loves most. There is no practical reason why George should not still buy the farm with Candy, but emotionally it is another story. The dream is dead as well as Lennie; perhaps George, the practical realist, knew it would end this way all along.

Lennie

Behind him walked his opposite, a huge man, shapeless of face, with large, pale eyes, with wide, sloping shoulders, and he walked heavily, dragging his feet a little, the way a bear drags his paws. His arms did not swing at his sides, but hung loosely and only moved because the heavy hands were pendula.

Lennie is a half-wit, a simpleton, but also, as Slim and Curley's wife point out, a 'nice fella'. He is in effect a child's mind in an immensely strong man's body, and his tragedy is that his mind has never learnt how to control his body. He is amazed and upset when his mice and his puppy die, unable to believe that they are so fragile, and unable to realise that it is not their fragility but his strength that is to blame. After his strength his most noticeable feature is his innocence, an innocence so transparent and obvious that the reader cannot help but sympathise with him, and feel for him the same affection that George obviously feels. He is described in animal terms quite often by Steinbeck, but this does nothing to lessen the degree of humanity that he shows. It is that, like a wild animal, his mind and body cannot cope with the complexities of modern living. The only way he can survive is to be like a tame dog, always tethered to his master George, and never let out of his sight. Yet Lennie is not totally straightforward. He has a type of animal cunning that he can bring into play, as when George loses his temper with him at the start of the novel. Knowing that George will feel guilty about his loss of temper, and about taking away Lennie's mouse, Lennie plays on George's feelings of guilt:

Lennie avoided the bait. He had sensed his advantage. 'If you don't want me, you only jus' got to say so, and I'll go off in those hills right there—right up in those hills and live by myself. An' I won't get no mice stole from me.'

As a result of this, Lennie gets the sympathy he wants from George. Lennie is cunning and aware in another sense. His instincts tell him that the ranch is a bad place to be:

> Lennie cried out suddenly: 'I don' like this place, George. This ain't no good place. I wanna get outa here.'

Two aspects of Lennie's characterisation have been criticised: his holding on when frightened, and the two visions he sees at the end of the book. The holding on appears three times in the book—at Weed, with Curley's hand, and with Curley's wife—and the argument has sometimes been raised that retarded people like Lennie do not normally do this, but are more inclined to let go when frightened. This is not a valid point of view. Steinbeck is not describing the average retarded man, but one in particular. If that one happens to have a reaction whereby he holds on to things when frightened the reader is quite prepared to accept this, as long as it is at least possible. The other criticism, that one which attacks Lennie's visions, is more valid. This fantasy element does not fit in with the rest of the novel in content or tone, is not particularly powerful, and is unreal. Lennie's limited intellect has enough trouble speaking at all, and it is inconceivable that he could give his own voice to two people, and construct a dialogue. Critics may well be right when they cite these visions as being the result of Steinbeck's youth and inexperience when he wrote *Of Mice and Men*. It is only a minor blemish on an intensely moving and sympathetic portrait. Perhaps the best epitaph for Lennie is provided by Slim: 'He ain't mean'.

Slim

A tall man stood in the doorway. He held a crushed Stetson hat under his arm while he combed his long, black, damp hair straight back. Like the others, he wore blue jeans and a short denim jacket. When he had finished combing his hair he moved into the room, and he moved with a majesty only achieved by royalty and master craftsmen. He was a jerkline skinner, the prince of the ranch, capable of driving ten, sixteen, even twenty mules with a single line to the leaders. He was capable of killing a fly on the wheeler's butt with a bull whip without touching the mule. There was a gravity in his manner and a quiet so profound that all talk stopped when he spoke. His authority was so great that his word was taken on any subject, be it politics or love. This was Slim, the jerkline skinner. His hatchet face was ageless. He might have been thirty-five or fifty. His ear heard more than was said to him, and his slow speech had overtones not of thought, but of understanding beyond thought. His hands, large and lean, were as delicate in their action as those of a temple dancer.

The above passage is by far the longest opening description given to any character in *Of Mice and Men*, a fact which illustrates how deeply interested Steinbeck was in Slim. It leaves little to be said about Slim, as the rest of the book merely emphasises the points made above, and brings in nothing new. It is Slim who understands the bond between George and Lennie, and comes to a correct character judgement of Lennie. Slim is the only character who understands why George has to kill Lennie, and what he feels when he has done so. His words, 'You hadda, George. I swear you hadda', say all that there is to be said after the incident.

There are some question marks hanging over the portrait of Slim. Critics have questioned what he is doing in the bunk-house at all if he is such a princely and dignified figure. Others have said that he is idealised, too perfect a figure to be credible. The description Steinbeck gives of him could be used without disrespect of an elder statesman, a great teacher, or a philosopher, and it may seem ludicrous that it is in fact applied to a ranch-hand, albeit a skilled one. Slim seems to be a product of Steinbeck's desire to show nobility of mind and purpose can be found in all sections of society; it may also be part of Steinbeck's campaign to raise the popular reputation of migrant workers, a campaign that he brought to its finest fulfilment in *The Grapes of Wrath*.

Candy

The door opened and a tall, stoop-shouldered old man came in. He was dressed in blue jeans and he carried a big push-broom in his left hand.

Candy has lost his right hand in a farm accident, and is now reduced to the meanest job on the ranch, that of 'swamper'. His function in the novel is to show the reader what happens to an old man beset by physical disability, loneliness, and rejection. He is a pathetic figure. He has lost all control over his life, and can only pass his time by being subservient to others, and getting his own back on them by gossip. Only twice in the novel does he stand up to people: once when he joins in the attack on Curley, and again when he tells Curley's wife what he thinks of her. In each case his defiance is short-lived, and serves only to make him seem more pathetic. Yet the reader is also shown how little it would take to revitalise Candy—just ten acres and a few animals are all that is needed to give him confidence and a spring in his step. He provides a parallel to George and Lennie, in that he clings to his dog as they do to each other. The dog's death reveals that Candy is a human being with all the human feelings and emotions, and as such should not be lightly dismissed; the incident where it is shot introduces Carlson's gun, which is vital for the ending of the story. It is also the dog that indirectly brings Candy in on the dream, for its death is what ensures his presence in the bunk-house when he hears George and Lennie talking about their plans for the little farm. Candy is one of the best examples of Steinbeck's compassion and sympathy for the old, the weak, and the down-trodden.

Crooks

This room was swept and fairly neat, for Crooks was a proud, aloof man. He kept his distance and demanded that other people kept theirs. His body was bent over to the left by his crooked spine, and his eyes lay deep in his head, and because of their depth seemed to glitter with intensity. His lean face was lined with deep black wrinkles, and he had thin, pain-tightened lips which were lighter than his face.

Like Candy, Crooks is an example of Steinbeck's compassion, and a further illustration of the way in which loneliness can corrupt and destroy a man. He has a double burden in that he is not only a cripple, but also a negro in a society that will not recognise negroes as anything approaching an equal. The true horror of his situation is revealed when Curley's wife crushes him when he tries to stand up to her, for no negro can hope to win against a white man or woman. Yet, if Steinbeck is compassionate, he is also fair. Crooks is not treated badly by the other ranch-hands, is described as a 'nice fella' by Candy, and is given a room on his own, even though it is right by a manure heap. He only appears two-thirds of the way through the story, and his function is to forewarn the reader and prepare him for the imminent destruction of George's and Lennie's dream by his cynicism and lack of faith. He has seen it all before, and knows what these dreams come to.

Curley

At that moment a young man came into the bunk-house; a thin young man with a brown face, with brown eyes and a head of tightly curled hair. He wore a work-glove on his left hand, and, like the boss, he wore high-heeled boots.

Curley has few redeeming features. He is a spoilt, restless young man with a grudge against the world:

> 'Curley's like a lot of little guys. He hates big guys. He's alla time picking scraps with big guys. Kind of like he's mad at 'em because he ain't a big guy.'

He has had some success as an amateur boxer, and boxing has become an obsession with him, so much so that every person he meets is seen as a possible opponent. He makes obscene allusions to his young wife, and goes to the brothel on Saturday nights, and then thinks he has a right to complain when his wife seeks to take her pleasures in a similar vein. He is obsessive about her, a laughing stock amongst the men for his continual hurrying after her in order to check that she is behaving herself, and is hated by her. He is not unintelligent, and has a form of cunning, but it is his inability to control his wife that brings about the tragedy in the novel, just as much as it is Lennie's nature; both are to blame. Curley is a man bordering on evil, and the most unpleasant and unattractive character in the book.

Curley's Wife

> She had full, rouged lips and wide-spaced eyes, heavily made up. Her finger-nails were red. Her hair hung in little rolled clusters, like sausages. She wore a cotton house dress and red mules, on the insteps of which were little bouquets of red ostrich feathers. 'I'm looking for Curley,' she said. Her voice had a nasal, brittle quality.

Curley's wife (her real name is never revealed) is a pathetic figure, as much a victim of loneliness as any in the novel. She has married Curley without really knowing him, out of spite against her mother and as a result of being disappointed about a supposed invitation to go to Hollywood, and finds him boring and unpleasant. She is a 'tart', but not really evil, and her punishment in the book outweighs any crime she may have committed. There is even a possibility that she could have been a loving wife had she met the right man. As it is, she is the only woman we see on the ranch, and she wanders in and out of the bunk-house, forever chased by Curley and flirting with the men. Her behaviour is not attractive, but even here Steinbeck's compassion shines through. In death her face is wiped clean of its recent experiences, and she appears as a young girl again, sweet and innocent:

> Curley's wife lay with a half-covering of yellow hay. And the meanness and the plannings and discontent and the ache for attention were all

gone from her face. She was very pretty and simple, and her face was sweet and young. Now her rouged cheeks and her reddened lips made her seem alive and sleeping very lightly.

Even Candy's initial response to her as the destroyer of the dream ('You God damn tramp') changes as he looks at her dead in the hay to the more affectionate, 'Poor bastard'.

Minor characters

The Boss is 'a little stocky man'. Little is known about him. According to Candy he is 'a pretty nice fella. Gets pretty mad sometimes, but he's pretty nice.' He buys whisky for the hands at Christmas, and it may be that his wife is dead, as nothing is heard of her in the book.

Carlson is a 'powerful, big-stomached man', a ranch-hand and the one who objects to the smell of Candy's dog, eventually shooting it. It is his Luger pistol that George uses to shoot Lennie.

Whit is a young ranch-hand, the one who finds the letter to a magazine written by an ex-worker at the ranch. He is sent into the town to fetch the deputy sheriff after the murder of Curley's wife.

Style

An author's style is the way he uses words and phrases, or, in the simplest of terms, the way he writes. It can include such matters as his choice of words, the length of his sentences, the metaphors and similes he uses, his use of dialogue, and the frequency and content of his descriptive passages.

There are two styles in *Of Mice and Men*. One is descriptive and almost poetic in its intensity, the other down-to-earth and colloquial. Not the least of Steinbeck's achievements in the book is to blend these two styles together with almost complete fluency.

The descriptive style owes its success to a number of features, not the least of which are Steinbeck's minute observation of nature and his gift for unusual metaphors and similes. The latter is evident when he describes the head of a water-snake as being 'like a little periscope'. At first reading, this simile might seem totally out of place. A periscope is a man-made product of steel and glass, part of a machine designed for war, and found at sea, not in the confines of a small pool in a river. Yet the image does work. It is startling and unexpected, and so focuses the attention of the reader on what is being described. Visually the two images are linked, with the upright head of the snake and the upright periscope ploughing silently through the water being very similar. The snake's eyes are in its head, just as the periscope is the eye of the submarine. A submarine is a machine of death, but so perhaps is the snake, its head poking up to hunt for food among the shallows. The more the image is examined the more it seems apt and fitting. It also shows Steinbeck's ability to look behind and beyond his characters, his realisation that nature never stops moving even when man is present. The snake glides through the water whilst George and Lennie are talking, the reeds jerk, and the sycamore limbs rustle in the breeze.

Light is used often by Steinbeck, particularly in his descriptive passages. For instance, the light flaming on the top of the Gabilan Mountains is a recurrent image in the book, and Steinbeck is also fascinated by sunlight. He describes the light in the bunk-house:

> At about ten o'clock in the morning the sun threw a bright dust-laden bar through one of the side windows, and in and out of the beam flies shot like rushing stars.

This same bar of sunlight later achieves symbolic proportions when Curley's wife stands in the doorway and blots it out, perhaps a prophecy of what her role in the novel is to be. Later, the 'tin-shaded electric light' in the bunk-house is used to emphasise the artificiality and cheap tawdriness of the life the ranch-hands lead. The 'meagre yellow light' in Crooks's room also suggests his misery and weakness. The sunlight in the barn, which grows softer after the murder of Curley's wife, is a major element in Steinbeck's evocation of atmosphere. Here again Steinbeck uses the background of nature to convey the right mood. While Curley's wife lies dead in the hay, a pigeon flies in and out of the barn, and Slim's mongrel dog slinks past and into her nest when she catches the smell of death. These movements emphasise the stillness of the girl, and increase the feeling that her body is an empty shell, only now finding the peace it has craved all along.

Steinbeck also has an acute ear for everyday sounds, to colour his descriptions and give them the atmosphere of reality. The distant clang of horseshoes in the yard, the far-off shouts on the highway, the rustling of the horses in the barn, all these are used to place the reader in the scene and persuade him that he is an eye-witness of all that takes place.

Much of *Of Mice and Men* is written in the vernacular, slangy, and colloquial language of the ranch-hands. The only adjective that Candy seems to know is 'pretty', and lice are described at various times as 'grey-backs', 'bugs', and 'pants rabbits'. Double negatives abound; a random choice of page has 'Ain't got no relatives nor nothing' (possibly a treble negative?), 'Don't spen' nothing', 'I can't swamp out no bunk-houses', and 'they won't do nothing like that'. Slang and swear-words are found on every page, and throughout the book 'and' is usually 'an' ', 'just' is 'jest', 'sat' is 'set', 'ask' is 'ast', and 'full of' is 'fulla', to name but a few. Despite this, the dialogue is remarkably easy to read. It is vigorous, realistic, and occasionally very evocative. It has the rhythm and the feel of real life.

Of Mice and Men is not a comic novel, but Steinbeck is too much of a realist to leave humour completely out of his story. There is undoubtedly comedy in Slim's first words, after he has been built up by Steinbeck as a prince among men. This almost ecstatic praise is followed by Slim saying, 'It's brighter'n a bitch outside', a line which brings the reader back down to earth with great rapidity. There is the lightly amusing description by Candy of the man who used to work at the ranch and who had an obsession over cleanliness, and Candy's wide-eyed amazement at a man who washes his hands 'even *after* he ate'. Even Crooks has a sense of humour, albeit a cynical one. Candy thinks Crooks's room is cosy, and implies that he is lucky:

'Sure,' said Crooks. 'And a manure pile under the window. Sure it's swell.'

There is heavy irony in this.

The two aspects of Steinbeck's style have been described as 'jewelled metaphors' and the 'practical language of fact'. Only twice does his control seem to slip, in the passage where time seems to stand still in the barn, and in the invention of Lennie's visions, but these are minor blemishes on a novel that combines some extremely moving and evocative writing with a hard edge of reality and conviction.

Steinbeck's dramatic style

Steinbeck is often said to have a dramatic style, meaning that *Of Mice and Men* is similar in some respects to a play, particularly in the area of its style. The similarities are not difficult to see. Much of the action is carried forward by dialogue, there are only six 'scenes' in the book, the settings for which could easily be reproduced in a theatre, and the novel also has only a few characters. Light is used liberally in the descriptive passages to evoke atmosphere, and of course light is one of the technical aids most easily available to a theatre director. Steinbeck describes his characters through their physical appearance and their speech, which is again a technique well suited to the theatre. Indeed, the one exception to this, Slim, has been said to be characterised (in the first paragraph which Steinbeck devotes to him) by means of a 'stage-direction', the instructions to director and actor that an author includes in the script of a play. It is true that this paragraph on Slim does read a little like a stage-direction, except that it is longer than we would normally expect to find in a play. Steinbeck relies quite heavily on sound effects in *Of Mice and Men* (the clang of horseshoes, the rustling of the horses), and one passage in particular is very reminiscent of the theatre. This is when the hands arrive back from the fields for lunch on George's and Lennie's first morning at the ranch. In the theatre, a director would not be able to show the audience the great wagons and mules pulling up outside, as he would have neither the animals nor the space to do this. He would instead use the traditional stage device of 'sounds off', where sound-effects create the illusion for the audience that there really are men, machines, and animals drawing up outside. This is precisely what Steinbeck does, even though as a novelist there is nothing to stop him taking the reader outside and seeing for himself. Thus he writes:

A sound of jingling harness and the croak of heavy-laden axles sounded from outside. From the distance came a clear call. 'Stable Buck—ooh, sta-able Buck!' And then: 'Where the hell is that God damn nigger?'

The book could also be described as dramatic in the sense that all the sections except the first one culminate in a moment of tense climax. In Section 2 it is the scene with Curley, in Section 3 the shooting of Candy's dog, in Section 4 the argument between Candy, Crooks, and Curley's wife, in Section 5 the death of Curley's wife, and in Section 6 the shooting of Lennie. Such moments of climax make excellent material for a live audience, and would transport very easily to the theatre.

Of Mice and Men, therefore, has many of the ingredients of a play, and it is not difficult to see why it was adapted so successfully for the theatre. This is not to say that Steinbeck was consciously writing for the theatre when he wrote the novel; had he been doing so, he might just as well have produced a play and not a novel. It is simply that his natural style as it evolved was quite close to some of the techniques of writing for the theatre, a fact which is equally evident in *The Grapes of Wrath* and many of his other works. A certain amount of caution, however, needs to be exercised over the use of the word 'dramatic'. Certain critics use it rather loosely to convey the tension and excitement of the novel, and not the theatrical nature of its style; there is no great harm in this, as the novel is both tense and exciting, *and* theatrical, but the examination candidate should be aware which meaning he intends when he uses the word.

Part 4

Hints for study

Points to select for detailed study

There are certain passages in *Of Mice and Men* which should be studied in greater detail than that afforded the rest of the novel. All the passages reproduced so far in this work belong to this group; additional passages are as follows.

The opening part of Section 1 (the description of the area south of Soledad) is one of the best illustrations of Steinbeck's descriptive technique, and should be studied in conjunction with the opening passage of the final section. In particular, the reader should notice the changes that Steinbeck introduces into the description, in keeping with the darker and more sombre mood of the latter passage. The whole of the first section should be studied in detail, because it is full of significant detail, notably about the characters of George and Lennie, and their dream. In Section 2, page 27 (the first entry of Curley) is a dramatic moment, and introduces a character who will exert a major influence on the plot. Pages 31 and 32 (the first appearance of Curley's wife) are significant for the wealth of detail they provide about Curley's wife.

Pages 38 to 41 (in Section 3) reveal a great deal about George, Lennie, and their relationship, and perhaps also something about Slim. Pages 46 and 47 (the wait whilst Candy's old dog is shot) show Steinbeck's mastery of describing group situations, and are further examples of Steinbeck's flair for writing dramatically. Pages 53 to 55 (Section 4) give details about the farm George and Lennie hope to buy. Pages 57 to 60 give another dramatic moment, the fight between Lennie and Curley, and act as a good base from which to study Steinbeck's handling of action scenes.

Candy's outburst on page 69 ('Candy cried: "Sure they all want it . . ."') is a useful paragraph in that it shows the dream from another viewpoint than that of George and Lennie. Page 73 has Curley's wife reducing Crooks to a cringing slave, a good passage to illustrate the theme of racial prejudice in the novel.

The first few paragraphs of Section 5 are another good illustration of Steinbeck's descriptive technique and his ability to evoke a powerful atmosphere. Page 79, where Curley's wife unburdens herself to Lennie, supplies a great deal of insight into her personality and character. Candy's complaint about the destruction of the dream on page 85 is one of the most moving and poignant episodes of the whole novel.

The whole of the last section needs to be studied in detail, as the culmination of the tragedy.

The general points which require detailed study are given in the course of Part 3 of these notes. Of these, the ones that seem to concern examiners the most are the excess of clues given to the reader about what will happen at the end of the novel, the supposed lapses from excellence in the passage where time stands still after the murder and that in which Lennie sees his visions, Steinbeck's blending of two styles, his compassion for underprivileged people, and the portrait of Slim. However, all the topics discussed in Part 3 have been set as examination questions at one time or another, and all should be studied in detail.

Quotations

Any effective examination answer will contain quotations, as these are the main source of evidence available to an examinee. A good way of compiling a list of quotations that will satisfy the needs of an examination is to write down all the lines and passages quoted so far in this book, and then add to it the lines given below. This list will provide quotations for all the questions you are liable to be asked on *Of Mice and Men*. If you are allowed to take a copy of the novel into the examination with you, underline or mark the quotations in the text; if not, select and learn the most useful lines, remembering to learn them *exactly*, even down to the punctuation. You will be heavily penalised for misquotation, for the same reason that a lawyer would be heavily punished for falsifying evidence.

Section 1 (pages 7–20)

His huge companion dropped his blankets and flung himself down and drank from the surface of the green pool; drank with long gulps, snorting into the water like a horse.

This is a good illustration of Steinbeck's use of animal imagery in connection with Lennie.

Lennie looked sadly up at him. 'They was so little,' he said apologetically. 'I'd pet 'em, and pretty soon they bit my fingers and I pinched their heads a little and then they was dead—because they was so little.'

One of the warnings Steinbeck inserts into the early part of the novel about Lennie's strength and his inability to control it.

'Jesus Christ, somebody'd shoot you for a coyote if you was by yourself.'

Another warning about what will happen to Lennie.

Section 2 (pages 20–37)

'Bit I say he's a God damn good worker. He can put up a four-hundred-pound bale.'

Another illustration of Lennie's great strength.

'Well, I think Curley's married . . . a tart.'

A useful line for any character sketch of Curley's wife.

Both men glanced up, for the rectangle of sunshine in the doorway was cut off.

A symbolic image, hinting at the nature of Curley's wife.

'An I bet he's eatin' raw eggs and writin' to the patent medicine houses.'

George's straightforward disgust at Curley's antics gives rise to one of the mildly comic lines in the book.

Slim looked through George and beyond him. 'Ain't many guys travel around together,' he mused. 'I don't know why. Maybe ever'body in the whole damn world is scared of each other.'

Slim's comment on the loneliness of the ranch-hand.

Section 3 (pages 37–61)

'I seen the guys that go around on the ranches alone. That ain't no good. They don't have no fun. After a long time they get mean. They get wantin' to fight all the time.'

George's comment on the loneliness of the ranch-hand, and the effect that loneliness has on people.

'Jesus,' he said. 'He's jes' like a kid, ain't he?'

Slim's comment sums up Lennie.

Lennie breathed hard. 'You jus' let 'em try to get the rabbits. I'll break their God damn necks. I'll . . . I'll smash 'em with a stick.' He subsided, grumbling to himself, threatening the future cats which might dare disturb the future rabbits.

Steinbeck's repetition of the word 'future' emphasises how far away George and Lennie are from actually getting their little farm.

> Curley was white and shrunken by now, and his struggling had become weak. He stood crying, his fist lost in Lennie's paw.

An illustration of the terrible effect of Lennie's strength.

Section 4 (pages 61-75)

> Crooks bored in on him. 'Want me ta tell ya what'll happen? They'll take ya to the booby hatch. They'll tie ya up with a collar, like a dog.'

It is fear of this happening to Lennie that makes George shoot him.

> 'Everybody wants a little bit of land, not much. Jus' som'thin' that was his. Som'thin' he could live on and there couldn't nobody throw him off of it.'

Candy's expression of the reason behind the dream.

> Crooks had reduced himself to nothing. There was no personality, no ego—nothing to arouse either like or dislike. He said: 'Yes, ma'am,' and his voice was toneless.

This illustrates the crushing nature of racial prejudice, and the power that it gives.

Section 5 (pages 75-88)

> The afternoon sun sliced in through the cracks of the barn walls and lay in bright lines on the hay. There was the buzz of flies in the air, the lazy afternoon humming.

An illustration of Steinbeck's use of light and sound in his descriptions.

> 'All right, you guys,' he said. 'The nigger's got a shot-gun. You take it, Carlson. When you see 'um, don't give 'im no chance. Shoot for his guts. That'll double 'im over.'

These lines illustrate the viciousness of Curley.

> 'No,' said George. 'No, Lennie. I ain't mad. I never been mad, an' I ain't now. That's a thing I want ya to know.'

This is George's final apology to Lennie for what he has to do.

Effective arrangement of material

There are a number of basic rules which apply to the writing of an examination answer. The first is that of relevance. After having worked hard on a book, often over a period of months or even years, there is a great temptation to walk into an examination and write down absolutely everything you know, regardless of the question you are actually being asked. This will result in failure just as quickly as not knowing anything about the book at all. An examination tests not only what you know about a book, but also your ability to select the relevant facts from a mass of information. The second basic rule is that of planning, and the third is that you should always come to a conclusion in your answers, and present all sides of an argument. An essay that presents the facts for only one side of an argument is ineffective. You need to tell the examiner why he should take your point of view, but also why all the other possible points of view are less convincing. Remember also that there are two types of questions set in examinations on literature. The first is factual, and requires you to answer such questions as which character speaks certain lines, where in a book a passage is drawn from, and what are the basic details of the plot. The answers to these questions can be marked right or wrong, but the issues are not so simple in the second type of question, which is the general essay question. Here there is often no right or wrong answer, merely a number of possible points of view, any one of which might have a reasonable chance of being right. You gain marks not so much by the solution you choose to present as the right one, but by the force and skill with which you argue your choice. An example of an open-ended question is given below, in the first of the specimen answers: 'To what extent is *Of Mice and Men* a novel of protest?' There are a number of possible answers. Of course, it would be possible to write an answer that the examiner would immediately dismiss as being wrong, simply by presenting a view for which there was no supporting evidence in the text. But the student is more likely to choose to argue one of about three possible points of view, and find evidence to support all of them. The examiner therefore marks the answer not so much on the point of view expressed, but on the skill with which the writer forces his point home and presents his case. The student should also remember that in rejecting certain points of view in favour of others, he is not saying that the other points of view are totally wrong or misinformed, simply that the ones he has chosen to argue have more right in them, on balance provide a more convincing answer. An example of this type of balanced judgement would be an answer to the above question that said *Of Mice and Men* was not a novel of protest, as there were other features more dominant in it, but that it still had a considerable amount of protest within its pages. Such an answer is perfectly possible, and even admirable. It shows the examiner that the student is capable of a mature response to the novel that sees all sides of the question, not just the one he is answering.

Planning an answer

There are four stages in the writing of an effective plan; in an examination, the student will find that with practice these four stages need take no longer than five or six minutes, but they will be the most important minutes of the whole examination. Taking 'To what extent is *Of Mice and Men* a novel of protest?', the four stages of planning this answer are shown below. For the purpose of explanation the plan shown is very much extended; in an examination, the same four stages can be completed using much briefer note form.

(a) Note down rough ideas

When you first see a title and start to think about it, ideas that might be used in an answer will start to come into your head. These should be put down in note form, with no attempt as yet to organise them or put them into any particular order, as below:

Steinbeck known as a novelist who cared deeply about underprivileged people (as in *Grapes of Wrath*)
Protest in book against treatment of the old (Candy's dog, Candy)
not allowed to go into town —— racial prejudice (Crooks)
people not able to keep what they grow and harvest from the land – *men working for one landowner*
loneliness – *who isn't?*
Ranch-hands seem quite well treated – *seem quite content*
Protest against treatment of retarded people (Lennie)? – *men all kind to h.*
Main subject of novel George and Lennie, not protest
Outcome of story inevitable
No protest against ranch boss
Protest against Curley – *argumentative, looking for a fight*
The role of natural description in the novel
Of Mice and Men not a novel at all—more a *novella*
George and Lennie's dream of a farm real point of the novel – *dream*
Lot of compassion in the novel—is this its point?
Novel not intellectual or political

(b) Organise rough ideas into paragraphs

The notes above represent the first ideas that a student might have on seeing this question. They provide the best possible argument for planning an answer, because they show (albeit in note form) what the student would have written had he simply sat down and started writing immediately. You can see what this would have produced—some good ideas, but no logical development of the ideas, a lot of repetition, some irrelevant points, and an essay that jumps so rapidly from one point to another that the reader does not have the time to follow clearly what is being said. Obviously, a lot more work has to be done before these ideas can be turned into a good essay. The next stage is to group the rough ideas into paragraphs, and cut out the ideas that are either mentioned twice or which seem irrelevant. Possibly some new ideas will suggest themselves whilst this second stage is being carried out; your mind will still be turning over the implications of the question. Slot these ideas in where they seem most suited. It is also likely that some conclusions which can be drawn from the points you have discovered might suggest themselves. New ideas or conclusions have been put in italics in the plan below, to enable you to spot them more clearly.

(1) The novel contains protest at— treatment of the old (Candy, his dog)

 — racial prejudice (Crooks)

 — people not being able to keep what they grow and harvest

 — loneliness

(2) No real protest against treatment of retarded people.
Protest against Curley, *but this is simply protest about one individual.*
No protest against ranch boss.
Ranch-hands seem quite well treated.

(3) Novel not really political or intellectual; *calling it a novel of protest makes it sound as if it were.*
It is also a novel about nature.

(4) It is really a novel of compassion, not protest.
About George and Lennie and their dream, not protest.
Destruction of the dream not a protest, just a picture of real life.
Steinbeck leaves reader to comment.

(c) Put paragraphs in order/write conclusion

If you look at the above paragraph scheme you will see that a number of things have been changed in it from the preliminary notes. Certain points have been omitted. The first idea in the rough notes (that Steinbeck cared deeply about underprivileged people) has been discarded from the main part of the essay, but could be used in an introduction to it. The point about the ending of the story being inevitable has also been left out, as it no longer seems relevant, as has the point about whether *Of Mice and Men* is a novel or a *novella*. The question does talk about the book as a novel, but fairly obviously this is not what the title is about. A surprising number of students, when faced with a question like this, clutch at straws and write the first thing that comes into their heads, without actually taking time to work out what the actual question they are being asked is.

Only when all the facts and ideas have been assembled and grouped into paragraphs can the student see what his conclusion should be, because it is only at this point that he can see which point of view he has the most evidence for. Many students have done badly in literature examinations because they decided instinctively to argue for one side of a case, and only half-way through found out that they had more evidence for the other point of view. An essay that suddenly changes course mid-way through its argument is never a good one.

An answer should always finish with the points of view in favour of your conclusion, and any facts or opinions that point to another viewpoint should be placed at the start of the answer. If the writer of the above plan decides to argue that the book is not a novel of protest, his paragraphs are in the right order; the opening paragraph deals with the point of view he does not wish to support, and the remainder put forward his own view.

(d) Write topic sentences/find evidence

Before actually writing the answer, each paragraph should be given a topic sentence. A topic sentence is the first sentence in a paragraph, and it states in a few words what the subject or point of that paragraph is. It is useful because it gives the reader an immediate grasp of what is being said in that paragraph, and because it allows the writer to check quickly and easily if what he is saying is relevant to the title; if the topic sentence is not a direct answer to the title, and if it reflects accurately the content of the paragraph, then the paragraph is not relevant.

The final stage is to find or remember quotations to back up, prove, or illustrate the points made in the answer. Occasionally students who have learnt many lines from a text get rather carried away, and produce examination answers that consist of quotation and little else. A good answer will have a quotation to back up every point that is made, but producing an essay that is two-thirds text is worse than useless. The examiner could gain as much by reading the book himself!

Below are four specimen answers to standard questions on *Of Mice and Men*. The first answer is the one that might have been written from the above plan. Bear in mind that these are only possible answers, and not necessarily the only ones that are right.

Specimen answers

To what extent is 'Of Mice and Men' a novel of protest?

The novel that many critics still think of as Steinbeck's best, *The Grapes of Wrath* (1939), was seen by many as a novel of protest against the conditions imposed on migrant labourers. Whilst there is an element of protest in *Of Mice and Men*, it is a very different novel from *The Grapes of Wrath*, and cannot automatically be classified as a novel of protest.

There is protest in the novel against the treatment of old people, racial prejudice, people not being able to keep what they help to grow, and loneliness. Candy and his dog illustrate the theme of old age. Steinbeck says that old people are thrown out like rubbish when they have outlived their usefulness. When Candy is too old to swamp out the bunk-house, he will be dismissed, with no one to care for him. In his own words, 'I won't have no place to go, an' I can't get no more jobs.' His old dog has been shot; perhaps it has put the dog out of its misery, but it has increased Candy's. Steinbeck seems to be demanding a more dignified treatment for old people, one that allows them to retain their self-respect. Much the same could be said of his attitude to negroes. Crooks is a victim of racial prejudice, even though the treatment he receives at the ranch seems not to be too appalling, merely some rude language and 'gettin' hell' from the boss sometimes. He is an intelligent man denied any outlet for his abilities, and a cripple as well. When Curley's wife threatens him, revealing the power that any white girl has over a negro worker at that time, he is crushed:

Crooks had reduced himself to nothing. There was no personality, no ego—nothing to arouse either like or dislike. He said: 'Yes, ma'am,' and his voice was toneless.

[handwritten annotations:] against treatment of old people / racial prejudice / not letting people what they grow / loneliness

Steinbeck obviously does not approve of the treatment Crooks receives.
Candy also seems to voice a protest against those who farm the land
not receiving its rewards:

'I planted crops for damn near ever'body in this state, but they wasn't
my crops, and when I harvested 'em, it wasn't none of my harvest.'

Above all the novel protests against loneliness and the effect it has on
people. As George says:

'I seen the guys that go around on the ranches alone. That ain't no
good. They don't have no fun. After a long time they get mean. They
get wantin' to fight all the time.

Yet the reader is told that all ranch hands do go around alone, and that
a pair travelling together like George and Lennie are almost unique. It
is loneliness that drives Curley's wife to her fatal conversation with
Lennie and her flirting, and loneliness that besets Candy and Crooks.

However, there are certain areas in the novel in which the protest
seems either very mild, or not there at all. There is no real protest
against the treatment of retarded people. It is true that George and
Crooks think Lennie might be locked up if he were handed over to the
authorities, but as the result of his not being locked up is that he
commits murder, it is difficult to blame society for wanting to do this.
No one can deal with Lennie, be it George or society, and rather than
protest there is sad recognition of the fact that there is very little that
can be done for Lennie. There is protest against Curley (George calls
him 'a son-of-a-bitch' and nobody has a good word to say for him) but
this is just protest about one individual, and not enough to colour the
whole novel. Nor is there any real protest about an obvious target, the
ranch boss; he seems a 'pretty nice fella', and is certainly not evil. The
ranch-hands seem quite well treated (there are no complaints about the
wages, food, or living conditions of any significance from George,
Lennie, Slim, Carlson or Whit), and fifty dollars a month was not an
inadequate wage in those days.

Of Mice and Men is not a political or intellectual novel. Calling it
a novel of protest makes it seem as if it might be, if only because most
protest novels attack society or political systems. There are complaints
in the novel, but as has been shown above, there are also large areas
of possible protest and complaint that have been left alone. The title of
the novel of protest would also give inadequate recognition to the
importance of the descriptions of nature in the book, which are one of
its most powerful features.

Of Mice and Men is really a novel of compassion, and a novel about a dream that two men have about a small farm of their own on which they will be able to live free and fulfilling lives. The novel is 'about' these things in the sense that they are the features which dominate it, and the features which call forth from the writer his most moving and powerful passages. Thus it is not a feeling of loneliness that dominates the book, but an awareness of the author's compassion for those who are lonely, as well as for those who are old and those who are disadvantaged. It is compassion that is most evident when Steinbeck writes movingly of Curley's wife, her dead face purged of its loneliness and worry:

> And the meanness and the plannings and the discontent and the ache for attention were all gone from her face. She was very pretty and simple, and her face was sweet and young.

It is compassion that is present when Candy finally realises that the dream is dead:

> His eyes blinded with tears and he turned and went weakly out of the barn, and he rubbed his bristly whiskers with his wrist stump.

Compassion touches every major character in the novel, except for Slim, who does not need it, and Curley, who does not earn it. The dream itself encompasses four characters (George, Lennie, Candy and Crooks), and stretches out to thousands of ranch-hands, if Crooks is to be believed:

> 'I see hunderds of men come by on the road an' on the ranches with their bindles on their back and that same damn thing in their heads. Hunderds of them. They come, an' they quit an' go on; an' every damn one of 'em's got a little piece of land in his head. An' never a God damn one of 'em ever gets it.'

Of Mice and Men is not a novel of protest; it is a novel of compassion, and a novel about two men with a tragic dream. To protest is to comment on life; *Of Mice and Men* presents the reader with a picture of life, and leaves him to comment.

To what extent can Steinbeck be said to have a 'dramatic' style in 'Of Mice and Men'?

Of Mice and Men was turned into a very successful play, as were a number of Steinbeck's other works, and won a Drama Critics' award. This fact alone would suggest that it has dramatic elements in it.

Although the book is not divided up into chapters, it does have six distinct sections in it, each of which could easily become a scene in a stage play. The setting for each of these scenes would be easily catered for in the live theatre. The first and last sections by the pool in the Salinas River could be suggested by a backcloth and suitable lighting, and the scenes in the bunk-house and the barn would be easily re-created on stage. There are ten characters in the book, an economically viable number for a theatre, none of whom present any great problems for an actor.

Probably more by accident than design, Steinbeck's style in *Of Mice and Men* is very dramatic, in the sense that it almost seems designed for the theatre. Much of the action and characterisation is carried forward by dialogue. Steinbeck hardly ever intrudes into the novel, but lets his characters tell the reader themselves about other characters, and their own personalities. The only exception is Slim, as Steinbeck does include a quite lengthy descriptive passage about him. Otherwise, there is usually a brief introductory physical description, such as an author might include in a play to help and guide the director, and then the personality of a character becomes clear through his actions and speech. This is precisely the technique used in the theatre, where the author can hardly ever speak directly to his audience. Each of the characters is identified by one or more physical features, and these features would quickly lead an audience to recognise and differentiate between the characters. George is small, Lennie huge, Carlson has a big belly, Candy a stump where his hand should be, and Crooks has a bent spine and is a negro. Curley is distinguished by his hair, his wife by her sexuality and youth, and the boss by his high-heeled boots. Whit walks as if he were still carrying invisible grain bags.

There are other areas where Steinbeck almost seems to be writing for the theatre, notably in his descriptive technique and provision of climaxes in each section. In his descriptions Steinbeck tends to point out the details of light quite frequently, as well as those of sound:

> It was Sunday afternoon. The resting horses nibbled the remaining wisps of hay, and they stamped their feet and they bit the wood of the mangers and rattled the halter chains. The afternoon sun sliced in through the cracks of the barn walls and lay in bright lines on the hay. There was the buzz of flies in the air, the lazy afternoon humming.

Lines of light are the easiest of all effects to produce in the modern theatre, and the sounds Steinbeck details would be equally easy. It would be difficult for a theatre to place live horses on stage; even in novel form, the reader does not see the horses in *Of Mice and Men*, but hears them instead. Live animals or large machines are also not easily placed on stage, and it is as if Steinbeck was thinking about this when he wrote about the arrival of the hands back for lunch on George and Lennie's first day on the ranch:

> A sound of jingling harness and the croak of heavy-laden axles sounded from outside. From the distance came a clear call. 'Stable Buck—ooh, sta-able Buck!' And then: 'Where the hell is that God damn nigger?'

Notice how the return of the workers, their machinery, and the yard itself are suggested merely by sound, without the reader ever having to actually see them. Steinbeck's arrangement of climaxes may seem less obviously helpful to an adaptation of the book for the theatre, but are no less useful. The reader of a novel can put down the book whenever he wishes; the audience for a play must stay in the theatre for the duration of the performance, or at least until an interval is called. The writer of a play therefore has to ensure that his audience are not overworked in the course of the play; moments of high tension must alternate with more relaxed periods, to enable the audience to catch their breath and build up to the next climax. A conventional structural pattern in a play is for each scene to build up to a minor climax, and for there to be a major climax at the end of the play. This is what Steinbeck provides in all but the opening section of his novel; this opening section sets the scene and introduces the two major characters, and as such follows an equally respectable dramatic tradition. A large number of plays have an introductory first scene. Sections 2 and 3 of the novel have double climaxes, two with Curley in Section 2, and the shooting of Candy's dog and crushing of Curley's hand in Section 3. Section 4 has a climax at the moment when Curley's wife crushes Crooks, Section 5 has the murder, and Section 6 the shooting of Lennie.

It can therefore be seen that *Of Mice and Men* is a thoroughly dramatic novel, in the sense that many of its techniques and features are those of the live theatre. It is not merely Steinbeck's style that is dramatic, but his whole approach to the book.

Are there any weaknesses in 'Of Mice and Men'?

There are a number of points in *Of Mice and Men* which are generally held to be weaknesses, at least in comparison to the strength of the rest of the novel.

The first of these is the supposed clumsiness with which Steinbeck prepares the reader for Lennie's killing of Curley's wife, and his death. It has been said that Steinbeck is clumsy in this area in that he provides too many clues about what is to happen, so that the build-up to the final incidents is laborious and heavy-handed. There are certainly a wealth of clues in the early sections. The reader is told in the first section that Lennie likes to pet mice, but that he kills them:

'They was so little,' he said apologetically. I'd pet 'em, and pretty soon they bit my fingers and I pinched their heads a little and then they was dead—because they was so little.'

Also in this section George tells Lennie prophetically that he would be shot 'for a coyote' if he were on his own, and the reader is prepared for trouble by George's insistence on Lennie remembering where to come back to if anything does go wrong. George's account of what happened in Weed and his frantic holding on to Curley's hand are obvious pointers to the future, as are his admiration for Curley's wife, her apparent interest in him, and his killing of his puppy. The reader is therefore not surprised when Lennie kills Curley's wife, but this in itself is not a weakness, rather a strength. If he were unprepared, the reader might question the credibility of what Lennie does (holding on in his manner is not a normal feature), thus reducing the effectiveness of the story. Also, the suspense and tension in the novel come not from wondering *if* Lennie will do something, but *when* he will do it, so the intensive preparation loses nothing of this.

All in all, it is possible to argue quite convincingly that the build-up to Lennie's murder and death is skilfully engineered by Steinbeck, and not at all clumsy or laborious. It is equally true to say that the reader does not know clearly what Lennie will do, as Steinbeck lays some false trails. Right until the very end, it is possible that there could be a sexual involvement between Lennie and Curley's wife. Lennie comments several times that she is 'purty', and the girl says to Lennie, 'OK, Machine. I'll talk to you later. I like machines.' It is also possible that the trouble might come more directly from Curley, instead of from his wife. Even after the hand-crushing incident has been hushed up, Curley could still decide to use it against Lennie. There is even a possibility that the trouble for Lennie could come as a result of a false rape charge from Curley's wife; this is what happened in Weed, and the girl has threatened this to Crooks. The ending of the novel is therefore not foretold with quite the certainty that some critics have suggested.

The other major areas singled out by critics as a weakness in *Of Mice and Men* are two passages at the end of the book. The first is a short paragraph that comes immediately after Lennie has left the barn following the murder of Curley's wife:

As happens sometimes, a moment settled and hovered and remained for much more than a moment. And sound stopped and movement stopped for much, much more than a moment.

It has been said that this poetic paragraph does not fit in with the style of the rest of the novel, which is realistic, full of colloquial language, and not in any sense fanciful. Much the same could be said of the second passage, which is that in which Lennie sees visions:

And then from out of Lennie's head there came a little fat old woman. She wore thick bull's-eye glasses and she wore a huge gingham apron with pockets, and she was starched and clean.

This vision of Aunt Clara speaks in Lennie's voice, as does the 'gigantic rabbit' which replaces her. This is quite a brave attempt to go inside Lennie's head, but it is not convincing, partly because Steinbeck has refrained from doing this with any other character. The visions also stretch the credibility of the reader. Lennie has so much trouble speaking for himself that it seems highly unlikely that he could manage a two-way conversation from within his own resources. Nor do the visions add greatly to our understanding of Lennie, except for adding a little pathos to his portrait.

Other minor criticisms have been made of the novel, such as that George does not have to shoot Lennie, that Slim is an unlikely character to find in the bunk-house, and that Steinbeck is too concerned with showing misfits and cripples. If these are blemishes on the novel, they are not major ones, and are so slight as not to be noticed by the majority of readers. Of the two main criticisms, it seems that one, the build-up to the novel's ending, is inaccurate, but that the other, Lennie's visions, is a weakness, possibly due to Steinbeck's relative inexperience as a writer at the time he wrote *Of Mice and Men*.

What contribution to 'Of Mice and Men' does Slim make?

Slim is described as a tall man with dark hair, and 'the prince of the ranch'. He is a 'jerkline skinner', a man who can control a team of horses or mules with only one rein to the leader of the team.

Together with George, Slim is the hero of the novel, someone who can be admired almost without reservation by the reader. His word is accepted as law in the bunk-house, and there is hardly a character who has a bad word to say of him. Steinbeck says that, 'His authority was so great that his word was taken on any subject, be it politics or love.' Even Curley seems to respect Slim. A character like this is needed to balance the number of more unpleasant characters there are in the book, such as Curley, Crooks, and even Carlson.

Slim is useful in the unfolding of the story because he draws crucial information out of George, and because his opinions on other characters in the novel are accepted by the reader as coming from someone with knowledge and authority. Steinbeck thus uses Slim to tell the reader more about the other characters, and influence their judgements of them. Talking to him, George reveals the details of what happened at Weed, which the reader must be told but which would have been difficult to convey with any degree of realism without a character like Slim for them to be told to. In this conversation George also reveals his own compassion and intelligence, as well as providing the reader with much background information about himself and Lennie. For instance, it is from this conversation that the reader learns about Aunt Clara, and how it was that George came to team up with Lennie.

It is Slim who provides comfort and support for George in his moments of crisis, as well as ensuring that Curley keeps silent about what Lennie did to him. It is Slim who recognises, with George, that Lennie will have to be shot after the murder. His support of George (his comment after the shooting is, 'You hadda, George. I swear you hadda.') fulfils another function. The reader might question what George does, perhaps wondering if it would not have been kinder to hand Lennie over to the authorities for professional treatment of his condition. The fact that an authoritative figure like Slim supports and believes in what George has done is a vital factor which helps to ensure the reader's continued sympathy for the action.

Slim is also used by Steinbeck to direct the way the reader thinks about Lennie. After hearing the story of his life, Slim's verdict on Lennie is 'He ain't mean'. Slim is reassuring himself when he says this, but he is also reassuring the reader. Lennie is retarded, potentially dangerous, and eventually a murderer. The story requires that the reader feel some sympathy towards him, but this sympathy would quickly be lost if Lennie were to appear malicious, or in any way aware of the damage he does. Slim's lines come from a man whose judgement is respected, and so unobtrusively guide the reader's response to Lennie.

It has been suggested that Slim is too idealised, and out of place in the bunk-house. Whatever the truth of this, there is little doubt that Slim represents a type of person for whom Steinbeck felt personal admiration. He respected the skilled worker, the man who was a doer rather than a thinker. He makes a significant contribution to *Of Mice and Men*, particularly in influencing the reader's judgement of characters and revealing more about them.

Questions

1. How improbable is *Of Mice and Men*?
2. Discuss the part played in the novel by: Carlson; Curley's dog; Whit.
3. How does Steinbeck persuade the reader that Lennie is 'a nice fella'?
4. What contribution does Curley make to the novel?
5. Does Steinbeck condone or condemn Curley's wife?
6. What are the main techniques for creating atmosphere that Steinbeck uses in *Of Mice and Men*?
7. Discuss Steinbeck's blending of two styles in *Of Mice and Men*.
8. How effective is Steinbeck's use of dialogue and colloquial language?
9. What is the theme of *Of Mice and Men*?
10. Would you describe *Of Mice and Men* as optimistic or pessimistic?
11. Would you agree that *Of Mice and Men* is 'a novel of compassion'?
12. Why does George shoot Lennie?
13. Discuss the allegation that the portrait of Slim is unconvincing and idealised.
14. Why does the dream of 'ownin' a piece of land' exert such a strong appeal over ranch-hands like George and Lennie?
15. 'There are too many misfits, cripples, and unusual characters of *Of Mice and Men* for it to be accurately described as true-to-life.' Discuss.
16. Discuss the theme of loneliness in *Of Mice and Men*.
17. In what sense, if any, could *Of Mice and Men* be described as a 'regional novel'?
18. Discuss Steinbeck's treatment of scenes of violence in *Of Mice and Men*.

Part 5

Suggestions for further reading

The text

The first edition of *Of Mice and Men* was published by William Heinemann, London, 1937 and by Viking Press, New York, 1937. The current edition, from which quotations are taken, is that published by Pan Books, London, 1974.

Other works by the author mentioned in these notes

The Pearl, Pan Books, London, 1970
The Grapes of Wrath, Pan Books, London, 1975
These are also available in several other paperback editions.

General reading

ALLEN, WALTER: *Tradition and Dream*, Penguin Books, Harmondsworth, 1965. This is a survey of British and American fiction from 1920 onwards, and it contains a very useful chapter on Steinbeck.

FONTENROSE, JOSEPH: *John Steinbeck: An Introduction and Interpretation*, Holt, Rinehart & Winston, New York, 1963. One of the 'American Authors and Critics' series, this is a sensible introduction to the work of Steinbeck.

FRENCH, WARREN: *John Steinbeck*, Twayne, New York, 1961. One of the 'United States Authors' series, this is a book for the advanced student, but contains some very sound comment.

MURRAY DAVIS, ROBERT (ED.): *Steinbeck: A Collection of Critical Essays*, 'Twentieth Century Views', Prentice Hall (Spectrum Books), New Jersey, 1972. Another book for the advanced student in which the editor's introduction gives a useful survey of the state of Steinbeck criticism. There is an excellent essay on *Of Mice and Men*.

STEINBECK, ELAINE, AND WALLSTEN, ROBERT: *Steinbeck: A Life in Letters*, Heinemann, London, 1965. This is absolutely essential reading for all students. It is the record of Steinbeck's correspondence from his early days right up to his death. It gives a fascinating insight into his character, the way he thought, and his attitude to his own writing.

WATT, F.W.: *John Steinbeck*, Oliver & Boyd, Edinburgh, 1962; Grove Press, New York, 1962. One of the 'Writers and Critics' series, this is a well-written and readable introduction to Steinbeck criticism.

The student who requires a quick introduction to Steinbeck may find *The Portable Steinbeck*, Viking Press, New York, 1971, useful. Although this can be difficult to find, it is quite a good anthology, with selections from Steinbeck's works. Good as it is, it is no substitute for reading the original works.

The author of these notes

MARTIN STEPHEN was educated at Uppingham, the University of Leeds, and the University of Sheffield. He is at present Second Master of Sedbergh School, and was previously a housemaster and teacher of English at Haileybury College. He is the author of *An Examinee's Guide to English Literature,* the York Handbooks *An Introductory Guide to English Literature* and *Studying Shakespeare,* six titles in the York Notes series, and two books on military history; and is the editor of a new anthology of poetry of the First World War. He has made several appearances on radio and television as a folk musician, and has also worked as a professional artist. He is married with three children.